CHIEFTAIN
MAIN BATTLE TANK

1966 to present

THE TANK MUSEUM

First published in September 2016
Reprinted in October 2017

A catalogue record for this book is available from the British Library.

ISBN 978 1 78521 059 4

Library of Congress control no. 2016930198

Published by Haynes Publishing,
Sparkford, Yeovil,
Somerset BA22 7JJ, UK.
Tel: 01963 440635
Int. tel: +44 1963 440635
Website: www.haynes.com

Haynes North America Inc.,
859 Lawrence Drive, Newbury Park,
California 91320, USA.

Printed in Malaysia.

Copy editor: Michelle Tilling
Proof reader: Penny Housden
Indexer: Dean Rockett
Page design: James Robertson

Acknowledgements

An especially big thank you must go to all the staff at the Tank Museum, Bovington, archive and library, who were unfailingly helpful and cheerful in their support and assistance. Other much-valued contributors to this work were:

Andy Brend (Chertsey)
Andrew Chapman (3RTR)
Les Dalton (11H)
Tony Debski
Simon Dunstan
Pete Elsdon (14/20H)
Andy Fisher (3RTR)
Mark Gilbert
David J. Hobbs (Fort Benning)
Jonathan Holt (Tank Museum, Bovington)
Robert Jacobs (3RTR)
Andreas Kirchhoff
Robert Lockie
Dave Lomax (3RTR)
David Moffat (4RTR)
John Muir (RAAC/3RTR)
Roddy de Normann (RH)
Ossie Osbourn (RE)
Keith Paget (4RTR)
M.P. Robinson
Johnnie Rose (2RTR)
Mike Rose (4RTR)
Richard Rose (14/20H)
Carl Schulze
Trevor Sly (RH)
Tony Stirling (17/21L and Tank Museum, Bovington)
John Tapsell
Chris Trigg
David Viccars (3RTR)
Geoff Wells (16/5L)
Stuart Wheeler (Tank Museum, Bovington)
David Willey (Tank Museum, Bovington)
Mike Williams MBE (3RTR)

CHIEFTAIN
MAIN BATTLE TANK

1966 to present

Owners' Workshop Manual

An insight into the design, construction, operation and maintenance of the British Army's Cold War-era Main Battle Tank

Dick Taylor

Contents

OPPOSITE The almost-universally hated and horribly uncomfortable 'bone domes', which got in the way of Chieftain crews when closed down, and which made the use of the sights and periscopes very difficult. *(Courtesy Andy Brend)*

Foreword

Maj Gen (Retd) Sir Laurence New, CB, CBE, CCMI

I was both honoured and delighted to be asked to write the foreword to this fascinating book examining the DNA of the Chieftain Main Battle Tank (MBT) – conceived in 1950, born in 1966 and expired in 1996. The author is every bit as remarkable as the tank. Joining the Royal Armoured Corps (RAC) as a 16-year-old junior leader in 1976, he progressed rapidly through the ranks, ending his service as a lieutenant colonel with a total of 13 operational tours under his belt. He is now a respected historian with a first class degree in History, an MPhil in Historical Research and an MA in War Studies. For anyone involved in weapons procurement his book is essential reading, if only to avoid some of the mistakes that we made.

For those of us who had to operate in Chieftain, the word 'unreliable' was seldom far from our lips. How could this be when the protection levels, firepower and cross-country mobility were so great an improvement on Centurion, which itself had been one of the best (if not the best) all-round tanks in the world? Dick Taylor identifies two main reasons. Firstly, NATO planners insisted in 1955 that because there was going to be a critical shortage of diesel fuel in war, tanks developed thereafter would have to be capable of operating with a variety of other fuels 'with a minimum of re-adjustment'. All the tank-producing nations in NATO ignored the imposition except Britain! Thus, a proven commercial diesel engine could not be prescribed for FV4201; a unique multi-fuel powertrain would have to be developed. Secondly, the consequent engine development, started in earnest in 1959, intended to provide an appropriate power-to-weight ratio for the overall weight of no more than the 45 tons as specified in the Operational Requirement. But by 1966, when it entered service, the fully

BELOW One of the Tank Museum Chieftains demonstrating the movement available within the Horstmann suspension; the two centre roadwheels are taking most of the weight and are at the limit of their travel upwards, whilst the first and last wheels are off the ground.

stowed Chieftain weighed 54 tons. Thus the entire powertrain, cooling system, gearbox and final drive would always be under strain. Unreliability was inevitable but the scale of it was still a shock. I was the Brigade Major of 20 Armoured Brigade in BAOR in 1968/69 when one of our three armoured regiments, the newly formed Blues and Royals, took to the Soltau-Lüneburg Training Area (SLTA) for the first time. They suffered almost total loss of their Chieftains, about 40 breaking down in ten days leaving only three operational. If it wasn't cylinder liners, piston failure, overheating of the TN12 gearbox or failing air cleaners it was something as simple as stripping fan belts. I commanded 4th Royal Tank Regiment (RTR) from 1971 to 1973, which included two major exercises in Germany and MEDICINE MAN 1, the first battlegroup to train on the Suffield training area. A tart description of the latter was that it was a Royal Electrical & Mechanical Engineers (REME) exercise which also involved the RAC! My vivid recollection in both Germany and Canada was of Chieftain drivers having spare fan belts immediately available (some round their necks!) so that breakdown time could be minimised! We just had to live with it.

After my command tour I paid a price for being critical – it became a case of poacher turned gamekeeper! First I was packed off to Israel for two years to learn all I could from the Israeli Army, fresh from their triumphs in the Yom Kippur War. By evolution, they had turned our obsolescent Centurions into the magnificent SHOT CAL MBTs, with which they had decimated the T55s and T62s of the Syrian forces on the Golan Heights. When the UK had refused to sell Chieftain to the Israel Defence Forces (IDF) – the full story is told within – they had started to develop their own tank, which became Merkava (the Biblical Merkava't Esh, Chariot of Fire). I was the first Brit to be allowed (twice, in fact) to crawl all over the prototype with General Israel Tal, its designer. It was he who had previously offered us much critical advice – to which we had listened – on how to improve Chieftain. Second, after my time in Israel I found myself in the Ministry of Defence (MoD) in a very hot seat as Colonel GS (Operational Requirements – Armoured Warfare). In that role, an early action with others

was to terminate the MBT 80 programme and grab the Shir 2, heavily modified, to produce Challenger. We tried to avoid the mistakes suffered in the procurement of Chieftain but only others can say if we succeeded. We had to telescope the development phase and paid a price in some areas, especially fire control, but we got Challenger into service at least five years earlier than we could have hoped for with MBT 80. With less urgency, and much more attentiveness to Armour Trials and Development Unit's (ATDU) constructive criticism, our successors developed Challenger 2 into an outstanding MBT. But that is another story.

In this book, Dick Taylor has put the Chieftain tank under the microscope, revealing the weaknesses and strengths in its DNA, its growing pains and its unredeemable shortcomings. Quite rightly, a lot of space is devoted to explaining both the L60 engine and the L11 120mm gun. There is much to learn here. Those who ignore history are likely to repeat it.

ABOVE Lt Col (later Maj Gen Sir) Laurie New, who commanded 4RTR on the very first BATUS MEDICINE MAN exercise in 1972.

Chapter One

Design and development

Chieftain was a tank whose development origins were rooted in the early 1950s, and yet which did not enter service until 1966. It served until 1996, however. The story of its design and development is not only fascinating in its own right, but can also be taken as an object lesson in the many pitfalls associated with such a complex engineering project.

OPPOSITE A 1RTR Mk 11 Chieftain reverses at speed in the 1990s; although equipped with modern systems through a process of upgrading during its 30-year service life, the tank struggled in its early years to achieve automotive reliability, and was generally considered to be underpowered, in stark contrast to its excellent armour and gun.

ABOVE The
'Defensive Slugger'
– a Conqueror. The
tank was well armed
and armoured, but
too large a target
and too heavy to be
agile on a battlefield.
Britain was keen to
find a way to put
Conqueror's firepower
and protection on to a
vehicle no larger than
Centurion, but with
better mobility – a tall
order!

Introduction

By the early 1950s the British Army was operating the best all-round tank in the world, the Centurion. Having finally learned the hard-won lessons of the Second World War, the Centurion was originally conceived as a heavy cruiser tank, but had evolved into what was sometimes termed a capital tank – one that had the right balance of firepower, protection and mobility to operate both in support of the infantry and to defeat enemy tanks. Its one real weakness was high fuel consumption which restricted its range, but it was well armoured, reasonably simple to use and to maintain, and capable of being upgraded. On the Mk 3 variant used in Korea it had an 83.4mm 20-pounder gun, and from the early 1960s it was further re-armed with the superb 105mm L7 gun. However, it was clear that the advantage that Centurion gave its crews could not last indefinitely; indeed, the British felt it necessary to put nine heavy Conqueror tanks into each Centurion regiment from 1955 as a direct response to the threat perceived by the thickly armoured Soviet heavy tanks, the JS-III and T10. (The initial assessment of the armour thickness of the JS-III was conducted by an officer using the only image of the tank available – on a postage stamp!) The Conqueror used a 120mm L1 gun, developed by the USA, which was meant to be able to defeat the Soviet tanks at long range, leaving the Centurions to deal with the less-well-armoured medium tanks, the T55s and T34/85s. The Conqueror was too large and heavy, though, being described in one official document as a 'defensive slugger', and operating a mixed fleet is rarely a good idea. The introduction of the 105mm gun-firing Armour-Piercing Discarding Sabot (APDS) ammunition went some way to redressing the balance, although it took six years from the idea being suggested to the first Centurions being up-armed.

In Britain, after the Second World War debacle of allowing private industry to design tanks to very loose specifications, governmental organisations were made responsible for such development, although of course in close co-operation with those industries who supplied components and built tanks. Centurion was proof positive that this worked, being designed by the Department of Tank Design (DTD). Despite this, Centurion was not really a revolution in tank development. Rather, it was an evolutionary conventional design that employed many of the features that the Second World War experience had proved to be necessary: reliability; thick, well-sloped frontal armour; a high-velocity gun capable of knocking out enemy armour and delivering high explosive (HE); an efficient radio system; good crew ergonomics; an all-round vision cupola; and an engine that delivered sufficient output to provide a good power-to-weight ratio. It was also, as its development showed, capable of being upgraded and improved. However, it could not go on being improved forever, and at some point it would need to be replaced. In the mid-1950s, concerns were expressed by the General Staff that the next Soviet medium tank, expected into service in 1963, would mount an 'improved 100mm gun', and that Centurion's advantage would then be reduced or even lost. As it turned out, the new Soviet T62 mounted a 115mm smoothbore gun, a considerable improvement over the T55's 100mm. Fortunately, work on a new tank had already begun, and it would eventually enter service in 1966 as the Chieftain MBT.

Tanks, of course, are not developed in a linear manner; rather, component and system designers are constantly evaluating new concepts and technologies, to see which might have potential for the future. Most are discarded, but some show enough promise to be developed sufficiently to be included – or at least not immediately discarded – in new designs. Chieftain turned out to be a fascinating mixture of evolutionary design that could be traced back directly to Centurion and its predecessors, with a range of revolutionary components and systems that were breakthroughs in tank design. It used exceptionally thick armour, particularly as it was officially a medium, not a heavy tank. The cast armour was well shaped and sloped at the front of the hull and turret to present a small turret profile and to increase armour effectiveness. Putting the driver in the centre of the hull in a reclined (supine) position allowed the overall height to be lowered, thus making it a smaller target but also saving weight. The semi-automatic gearbox made it easier to train drivers and was much less fatiguing for them. It used the emerging infra-red (IR) technology to equip the crew with a range of gunnery, driving and defensive aids for fighting at night. Fuel was stored in panniers along the sides of the hull to increase range. The 120mm bag-charge gun was a byword in long-range accuracy and penetration that led the world for over twenty years, and its ammunition was better protected than in any other tank. So, yes, it was a revolutionary tank, much loved by its crews, but cursed to this day with a reputation for mechanical unreliability, caused, somewhat surprisingly, by designing a bespoke engine for the tank, which in itself was an unusual approach. Why this was so, we shall discover in due course.

Chieftain's history really begins in 1950, a bare five years after Centurion's introduction and with a war in Asia that proved that the state of equilibrium between East and West was precarious indeed. The outbreak of the Korean War reinvigorated defence spending in Britain after five years of cuts, and in August 1950 the government decided to expand the army and to look more favourably on new equipment for it. In September 1951, the Treasury agreed in principle to a Ministry of Supply/War Office (WO) proposal to start the development of Centurion's replacement, as modern tanks were definitely needed to fight a Cold War that was now extremely hot, and might well spread to Europe. The war reinforced the need – already identified in the Second World War – for much improved tank designs, as a small nation like Britain needed to offset sheer numbers with technology, and tank crews were scarce, valuable assets that had to be protected.

The impetus caused by the Korean War led to a flurry of research projects by all the tank-making nations, leading to some frankly bizarre ideas, as well as to others which matured and then saw service. Luckily, by then Britain was blessed with experienced tank designers and innovative engineers. During the early phases of establishing what form the Centurion replacement might take – what today would be called project definition – a number of interesting but ultimately fruitless ideas were examined. For example, one idea that was seriously considered in 1953 was using a liquid propellant gun, in which a conventional brass cartridge case is not used, but rather a measured amount of propellant in liquid form is fed into the gun chamber before firing. As attractive as the idea was in theory, the technology of the day was not mature enough to make it work, in part because of the corrosive nature of the liquid as well as problems with the propellant reservoir and pump system; indeed, the idea remains of interest to this day, but even now it has still not been successfully developed. Another concept looked at in the early 1950s was mounting the gun externally in a cleft turret, using a design from the Allen-Bowden company of Warwickshire; the concept was sound in many ways but introduced a number of problems, not least of which was separating the turret crew from each

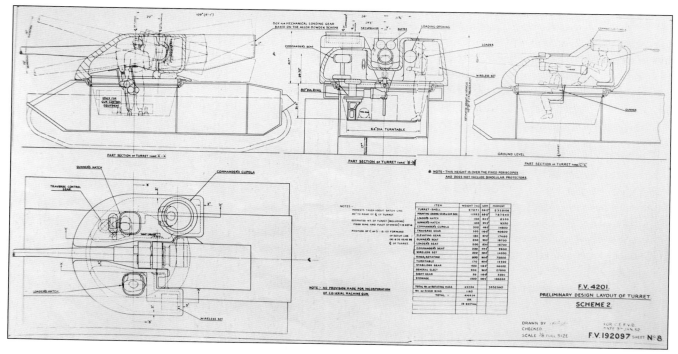

ABOVE A 1952 design proposal for an external gun in a cleft turret using the Allen-Bowden system: it was not found to offer sufficient advantages to warrant development and the turret alone weighed about 20 tons. Notice how short the hull is, in an attempt at keeping the overall weight down – this would have made the tank very difficult to steer.

RIGHT Size matters – particularly inside the turret where the space needed to load ammunition is critical. By using a separate projectile and bag-charge, the 120mm APDS could be made shorter and thus easier to handle than a 105mm equivalent using a conventional brass cartridge case (on the left).

other, as well as the increased armour surfaces – and therefore weight – that the design required, and so was not developed further.

By 1953 things were starting to take shape: it was recommended that the new medium tank should have a four-man crew, and would mount a conventional 105mm quick-firing (QF) gun, which could later be upgraded with a 105mm liquid propellant gun, plus Swingfire missiles which could be fitted at an unspecified future date when they came into service. (Discussions on how to mount Swingfire on to Chieftain under General Staff Requirement (GSR) 1007 of January 1961 – which never happened – were still taking place in 1963, and the project, which was never really feasible considering the sheer size of the missiles, was cancelled in 1964. As late as March 1961 there was another suggestion that a 20mm cannon could be mounted on to Chieftain, an unnecessary complication which had been tried and failed on Centurion, and which thankfully also came to nothing.)

Following provisional Treasury agreement in autumn 1953 for development funding,[1] on 15 March 1954 a specification was released by Lt Col A. Cooper, RTR, an RAC representative in the WO. This was known as the War Office

---

1 It has to be said unwillingly: a WO report noted that 'It was with some reluctance that in September 1953 the Treasury eventually agreed in principle to the development of FV4201.'

Policy Statement (WOPS) No 1. It set out the broad requirements for a new Medium Gun Tank – medium here referring to its projected weight, which in so many ways was to become the central and most problematic characteristic of the tank as it was developed. Initially called the Medium Gun Tank No 2, it soon became known by its Fighting Vehicle project number, FV4201; at this stage the name Chieftain had not even been dreamt of. The statement made it clear that the priorities for the new tank were to be:

- 'Highly effective gun power', followed by
- 'Capacity for sustained action on roads and cross-country', and then
- 'Best available armour within the overall weight limit.'

In order to be completely clear, it went on to state that 'Firepower and mobility must however be considered of prior importance.' Another statement forcefully made the point: 'On no account must we allow ourselves to be out-gunned' – the hardest lesson of the Second World War had clearly been learned. The weight limit was critical too, with an original intention to keep the weight down as much as possible. Indeed, the new medium tank was sometimes referred to as the 45-ton tank, and keeping the new tank on a diet was to become a preoccupation throughout its development, as we shall see.

It was then stated that the primary APDS projectile had to be able to defeat 'at least 100mm (later increased to 120mm due to the introduction of the T54) of armour plate sloped at 60° at 2,000 yards, with a 60% probability of a first-round hit using a rangefinder, against a target measuring 7½' × 7½". The secondary High-Explosive Squash Head (HESH) projectile should be able to defeat "at least 150mm",' assumed to be the frontal armour of the Soviet heavy tank. The APDS performance was essential whilst the HESH was desirable, meaning that the new gun was to be optimised for APDS performance. Some 60 rounds of ammunition were to be carried, 21 APDS or HESH and 39 HE. This specification – and remember that this was issued five years *before* the up-gunning of Centurion with the L7

105mm – led to three new gun designs being short-listed: a 105mm QF gun, a 105mm bag-charge gun and a 120mm QF low-pressure gun. The latter was primarily built for firing the slower HESH round, and was then developed into a higher-velocity weapon, but the APDS performance remained poor and the fixed ammunition was much too long for the limited space available in the turret. Despite this, the larger ammunition calibre showed the greatest promise, and it was assessed to be the most worthy of development in order to be able to defeat the expected Soviet armour thicknesses at the ranges required in the future. This was to lead, in a few short years, to the Chieftain's greatest attribute, the 120mm L11 gun.

The second priority, capacity for sustained action, was directly related to Centurion's biggest weakness, its lack of operational range. Centurion used the proven Meteor petrol engine, which was quite powerful but very thirsty. The problem that the engine designers faced was how to increase the range of the tank as well as producing sufficient horsepower to make it agile on the battlefield. The engine that was developed specifically for Chieftain was unfortunately to suffer from a series of problems of both power and reliability, which were to besmirch the tank's reputation throughout its service. In mobility terms, the new tank was to be at least as good

ABOVE The long-barrelled L11 rifled gun gave the tank unprecedented accuracy *and* penetration, the twin attributes needed for a successful anti-armour performance. However, the fire control systems needed constant upgrading to get the most from it.

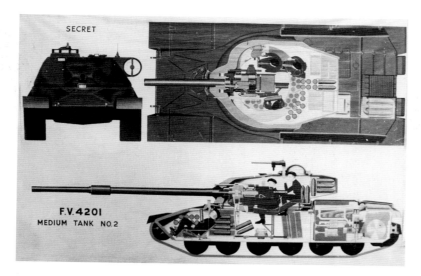

SECRET

F.V. 4201
MEDIUM TANK NO. 2

ABOVE AND BELOW
Drawings for FV4201 from the late 1950s, showing the proposed layout and the original 60° armour scheme on the hull and turret; this was later reduced to 45° in order to save weight.

as (and preferably better than) Centurion. In practice, this meant not so much giving it a high top speed as providing a stable gun platform across country (which, as well as allowing the stabilised gun to be used for shooting on the move, would also help to reduce crew fatigue), greater range, the ability to cross broken terrain, and a decent acceleration from a standing start in both forward and reverse.

The third priority was in many ways the perennial problem of tank design: to put the maximum armour on the tank, in the most effective places, without making the tank heavier than specified. In fact, what happened

with Chieftain also happened to many if not most other tanks: the armour scheme, once decided, remained quite fixed (with only one major concession made to reduce weight), but weight was constantly added on to the tank as new and more sophisticated systems were fitted. These included: bigger roadwheels; larger suspension units; new final drives; IR night-fighting equipment; very large fuel tanks; rubber pads for the tracks;[2] the nuclear, biological and chemical (NBC) pack; and, not least, a whole host of engine improvements and modifications including an increase in the length of the hull by around 4in to accommodate a major redesign of the engine. All of these prevented the tank achieving its original design weight of 45 tons. In order to protect the crew, the minimum armour thickness specified for the turret frontal arc – the place most likely to be struck – was 9.5in (240mm), a large increase when compared to the 6in on Centurion's mantlet; as it turned out, due to the shaping of the armour the maximum effective thickness of the Mk 2 turret casting was, in fact, a massive 500mm. The rear sides of the turret (*ie* aft of the main casting) were to have only 30mm of armour as they were much less likely to be hit. For the hull, the desirable figure was a maximum 15.25in

---

2 These alone added 1,125lb to the weight of the tracks, over half a ton.

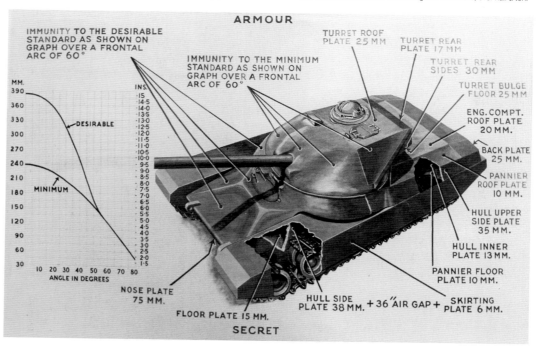

(388mm) for the main glacis casting (compared with 5in on Centurion and 10in on Conqueror), with a 75mm noseplate, 38mm hull sides and a 15mm floor.

In July 1957 the Treasury – as helpful as ever – suggested that the imminent up-gunning of Centurion with the 105mm L7 would remove the need for a new tank and, of course, the costs involved. The WO – subsequently the MoD – replied that a new tank was indeed necessary, in order to counter the threat of newer Soviet tanks expected in the 1960s, as the firepower advantage gained by the 105mm would be temporary. In December that year the MoD was considering the fact that co-operation with France might be advantageous in building a new tank, but the French were not interested in a collaborative project. Detailed design work started in 1957, and although the original drawings have yet to come to light it must have been at this stage that Chieftain really started to take shape – literally. In November, a revision to the requirements documents increased the gun elevation from +15 to –7°, to +20 to –10°, this enhanced capability at the expense of another increase in height and thus weight.

In May 1959, the Provisional Development Specification for MBT FV4201 was issued.[3] This updated the WOPS No 1 of 1954 and its later version WOPS No 2 of August 1958, and was able to more precisely define what

was required. This lengthy document is clearly recognisable as a description of an early Chieftain. In summary, it specified:

- Weight limit 100,000lb (45,359kg);
- 60 rounds of Main Armament (MA) ammunition – 20 APDS, 40 HESH/HE;
- The driver to be in the hull centre;
- A cast mantlet-less turret extending to 12in behind the centreline (roughly eight to four o'clock), remainder to be welded plate;
- Glacis and turret front to be impervious to the 'improved Soviet 100mm tank gun' at 700yd.

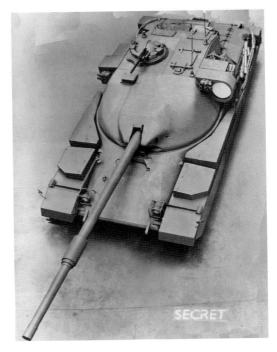

ABOVE AND BELOW
Taking shape: artists' impressions of FV4201, very similar to how the prototypes would look and clearly a Chieftain. The straight front to the hull nose would be replaced by a slightly angled one on the service tank, in order to give the taller driver a little extra legroom.

3 The new term 'Main Battle Tank' was being used in some official documents as early as May 1959, and in July 1960 the WO directed Leyland to cease referring to Medium Gun Tank No 2, and call it a Main Battle Tank instead.

ABOVE Inside the mock-up: although changes were made, the basic layout was established and is recognisable as a Chieftain. *(TM 6617F5)*

BELOW A drawing showing the very early turret layout, including the awful No 11 cupola and the M85 RG to the left of the 120mm breech.

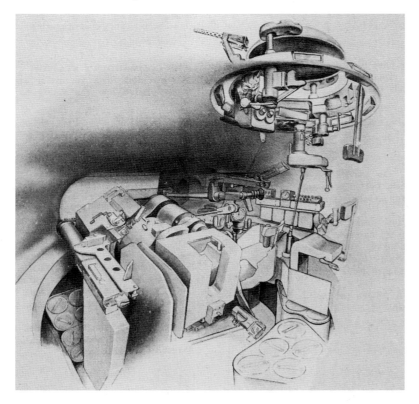

- .30 Coax MG.
- 85in turret ring.
- Water-jacket charge containers.
- 6-cylinder vertically opposed 2-stroke CI multi-fuel engine, developing 700bhp at 2,400rpm.
- TN12 semi-automatic gearbox.
- 28in-diameter roadwheels.
- Dimensions: Hull length 22ft 3in. Length gun front 32ft 10in. Length gun rear 30ft 4in. Width 11ft 4in. Height top of cupola 9ft 1in. Height turret roof 7ft 10in. Ground clearance 17in.
- Max speed 25.6mph.

Turning this more detailed specification into the new tank had already started; it was entrusted to Leyland, an experienced tank producer. Problems were encountered almost immediately with the complex turret design, and in order to prevent this delaying the appearance of the prototypes, Vickers-Armstrong (VA) had to be asked to step in to design the first version of the turret in September 1958. A wooden mock-up of the new tank was built in early 1959 by Leyland and exhibited at the Director Royal Armoured Corps (DRAC) Conference in December 1959. Senior officers had the opportunity to view the layout, and a number of suggestions were made – doubtless many of these were unhelpful and were discarded, but other sensible ideas were taken forward. At the same conference, the assembled officers were also introduced to a new concept – the MBT. It was explained to them that they would soon get used to this new NATO terminology, and that the Centurion replacement would be Britain's first MBT. Shortly after this, when the first prototype was complete and the second nearly ready, thoughts turned to giving the new MBT a name. Following the convention of giving Cruiser tanks names beginning with a C, 18 different names were considered by the RAC in March 1960, these were:

CAMBRAI	CARABINIER	CARDIGAN
CORNWALL	COBRA	CONDOR
CALIDON	CORUNNA	COUGAR
CUTLASS	CANBERRA	CONNAUGHT
CONQUEST	COURAGEOUS	CHIEFTAIN
CHAMPION	CAESAR	CHEETAH

The final decision seems to have been taken by the DRAC, Maj Gen Hopkinson, on 4 April 1960, and the now-famous name Chieftain was in regular use by April 1961. The newly named Chieftain made its first public appearance to the media and to many senior officers from other arms, on 24 October 1961 at Fighting Vehicle Research & Development Establishment (FVRDE), Chertsey in Surrey.

Prototypes on trial

On 16 April 1957, a contract (406/FV/17514) was issued for eight vehicles: six were for technical development of FV4201 and were the first prototype vehicles, identified by the prefix P. All six were built by Leyland at their works in Lancashire; the other two were FV4202 '40 ton Centurion' trial vehicles, plus one wooden mock-up of each type. The FV4202 was never intended to become a 'Super Centurion', as has sometimes been suggested, but was produced purely to rapidly develop concepts that were going to be used on FV4201, particularly the reclining driver and the cast mantletless turret, along with the early 105mm bag-charge gun. The development of the two FV4202 and six FV4201 by Leyland cost the taxpayer £639,724 – an average of £80K per tank.

A further six prototype FV4201 tanks were then ordered in June 1959; these were prefixed W, standing for WO vehicle, and were for user/ troop trials by the military. The factories that were to build the service tanks, Royal Ordnance Factory Leeds (ROFL) and the VA factory at Elswick, built three apiece. These vehicles had been approved on the basis of a predicted cost of £500K (which eventually ended up as £630K, an average of £105K each). Two examples (W1 and W3) arrived in Germany for user trials at the end of December 1962, one going to 1RTR and the other to 5RTR, their crews having already been introduced to the prototype tanks

RIGHT Two very new and shiny prototypes, one with a searchlight and the early tracks, the other with no searchlight but the padded tracks. The canvas turret covers and false hull front stowage boxes are only there to conceal the revolutionary shape. *(Courtesy Andy Brend)*

THIS IS THE
CHIEFTAIN

THERE has never been a tank like the Chieftain. It is faster and more mobile, harder hitting and harder to hit and of a more revolutionary design than any other tank in the history of armoured warfare.

One of its many outstanding features is its low silhouette, achieved by having the driver lie flat on his back and steer with the aid of a periscope.

Its very high velocity gun—an improved 120 mm —is the most powerful and accurate tank gun in the world, with a range of up to 20 miles, and its round is capable of piercing any known thickness of armour.

The Chieftain weighs only 47 tons—three tons lighter than the Centurion and 18 less than the Conqueror— but its armour is as strong as the Conqueror's. It is the fastest tank Britain has produced, having a road speed of more than 40 miles an hour.

The new tank is driven by a multi-fuel engine which runs equally well on low grade diesel oil or high octane aviation petrol.

Six of the eight Chieftains which have already been built—they are reputed to cost more than £60,000 each—will soon be sent to Rhine Army for troop trials.

MILITARY MIGHT ON SHOW

It was an impressive and heartening sight when the curtain was lifted on the Army of the future. On display were all the latest military weapons and, making their debut, some of the weapons and equipment which will soon be coming into service

THE world's most powerful tank, its huge gun emphasising its remarkably sleek and low silhouette, roared down the road. The *Chieftain*, Britain's fastest and most heavily armed new battle tank of a revolutionary design, was on show for the first time.

The *Chieftain*, which packs a bigger punch than either the *Conqueror* or *Centurion*, was making its debut at the Fighting Vehicles Research and Development Establishment at Chertsey in Surrey, during the biggest demonstration of Army weapons and equipment ever held.

ABOVE *Soldier Magazine* of January 1962 announced the appearance and official introduction of the new tank to its readers. It might be asked how many readers truly believed the claims of a 20-mile range from the main gun, and 40mph!

PRE-PRODUCTION VEHICLES – HISTORY

Vehicle (and registration)	Maker	Completed	History
P1	Leyland	18 Jan 60	Automotive prototype, no turret fitted initially. Limited running at Leyland before being shown to DRAC Conference in December 1959 in an 'incomplete state'; returned to FVRDE in January 1960. Road trials with engine governed to 1,800rpm first half 1960; by May 660 miles completed. June 61 gearbox failure. Used in submergence trials during 64. Destroyed in HESH firing trial Kirkcudbright Jan 67.
P2	Leyland	11 Apr 60	Automotive prototype, no turret fitted initially. Road trials with engine governed to 1,800rpm. Nov 60 cross-country trials, gearbox failure at 948 miles. Transmission testing Jan 64. Long Valley automotive trials in Feb 64, mileage 4,165.
P3	Leyland	Aug 60	GPMG trials Jan 62. Infra-red equipment trials Kirkcudbright Feb 62. Gunnery trials remainder of 62. GCE No 7 trials spring 63. Turret removed and fitted to W1 mid-63. GCE and RG trials Kirkcudbright Aug 63–Apr 64. New RG mounting trials May 68.
P4 (6424)	Leyland	Jul 61	ARGUS demonstration vehicle. RARDE '5 guns' trial Kirkcudbright. Gun jump and obscuration trials Jan 62. At ROFL for reworking Jan 64. By Feb 64, 40 miles completed. MBSGD trials Stoney Castle Feb 65.
P5	Leyland	Apr 62	Stoney Castle ranges GPMG trials Apr 62, Jul 62. GPMG coax MG trials Kirkcudbright 62. No 11 cupola trials Kirkcudbright Feb 64. Range target at Kirkcudbright
P6 (99SP23)	Leyland	Nov 62	Ventilation trials in hot chamber Jan, Feb 64. Used in snorkel trials. Now at Bovington Tank Museum.
W1 (00DA05)	ROFL	Mar 61	To FVRDE Mar 61. ARGUS demonstration vehicle. Fitted with improved engine. To RAC Centre Bovington for automotive trials 8 Jan 62. By end Feb 62, 331 miles on road and 305 miles X-country completed. Returned to FVRDE for inspection and reworking, then to BAOR 8 Jan 63 for troop trials. To FVRDE Apr 63, turret from P3 fitted. GCE trials completed by Feb 64.
W2 (00DA06)	ROFL	Apr 61	To RAC Centre Bovington with Windsor turret for automotive user trials 1 May 61 with 230 miles running-in on clock. By Nov 61, 542 miles on roads and 125 miles X-country completed. Returned to ROFL for rework to 'near-production' standard and fitting of gun turret Jun 62. Uprated suspension fitted with raised final drive and idler, Centurion roadwheels. Mk 3 powerpack installed FVRDE end 63/early 64. To RAC Centre Bovington for trials to Feb 64. At 5MAG Chertsey Mar 64, modified suspension and brakes fitted. 945-mile trial Mar–May 64 at Bovington. RAC Centre thereafter.
W3 (00DA07)	ROFL	Apr 61	To Kirkcudbright ranges 24 Apr 61. First live firing trials Kirkcudbright May 61. Returned to FVRDE 6 Jun 61 for 'essential mods'. To Lulworth ranges for firing trials 20 Sep 61. Returned to FVRDE Feb 62 for fitting 'latest engine'. Gunnery trials at Lulworth spring 62. To BAOR for troop trials 22 Dec 62. To FVRDE Apr 63. Ex-PALLOS demo vehicle Kirkcudbright Jul 63. No 15 cupola fitted in Dec 63 for trials at Kirkcudbright Feb 64. RAC Gunnery School 4 Sep 64 on.
W4 (00DA02)	VA (Elswick)	Dec 61	Straight from production to FVRDE for rework with Mk 2 engine, new gearbox and uprated suspension until Oct 62. Joint FVRDE/user 1,000-mile trial FVRDE 2 Nov 62. Completed 443 miles on test track and 501 miles X-country (with two new gearboxes). To RAC Centre Bovington 1 Jan–16 Mar 63 automotive trials. By June 1963 it had covered 3,252 miles. IR trials Oct–Dec 63. Jan 64 3,650 miles. To ROFL for reworking 17 Feb 64.
W5 (00DA03)	VA (Elswick)	Feb 62	Straight from production to FVRDE for rework until Dec 62. Early hull and suspension, M85 RG and No 11 cupola. To RAC Centre Bovington 18 Dec 62 for high mileage trial. Jun 63 padless track trials. By Jun 63 it had covered 4,001 miles, including 3,000 in less than two months. IR trials Oct–Dec 63. Reworked Nov 63. By Feb 64 over 6,000 miles completed. 120mm at end of useful life Jun 64, having fired 713 rds. In Jun 64 reported as having 'old modified long hull and suspension, old cupola, M85 RG'. RAC D&M School Sept 64 on.
W6 (00DA04 and 05MS99)	VA (Elswick)	Apr 62	To BAOR by early 63. Swapped with G1 as sales vehicle hence change of registration. Reworked for FRG Nov 63–Feb 64. FV434 trials Nov 64. FRG use from Jan 66 to 80, then exchanged with USA and in Fort Knox, then Benning.
G1 (01DC87)	ROFL	Jan 62	Intended for FRG but swapped for unknown reasons with W6. To Lulworth ranges for firing trials 15 Feb 62 to replace W6. Returned to FVRDE for rework to latest standard Jan 63. At FVRDE for reworking Feb 64. Ex-PALLOS demo vehicle Kirkcudbright Jul 63. At FVRDE for reworking Feb 64. RAC Gunnery School Jul 64 on. Now at Bovington Tank Museum.
G2 (01DC88 and 05MS98)	VA (Elswick)	Nov 62	Reworked for FRG Nov 63–Feb 64. FV434 trials Nov 64. FRG tank from Jan 66. Now at Aberdeen Proving Ground?
PP1 (12DM40)	ROFL	Dec 64	Very similar to production Mk 1. Expected ISD May 64, delayed to Dec 64. Larkhill trials May 65.
R1, R2	ROFL	Dec 70, Nov 72	Prototype ARV. R1 converted to Training ARV 1980.
E1, E2	ROFL	Dec 70, early 71	Prototype AEV(W). Both converted to Training ARV 1980.

Source: Development of FV4201 Chieftain by TLH Butterfield (AD Tracked Vehicles FVRDE) 1963; TM and NA records.

1. Steering brakes hydraulic supply tank
2. FIREWIRE
3. Auxiliary engine exhaust heat shield
4. Brake cylinder bleed nipples
5. Fuel return junction
6. Parking brake band return springs
7. Parking brake band
8. Main engine exhaust
9. Gearbox dipstick
10. Gearbox governor
11. Exhaust compartment louvres

Fig 35 Transmission compartment, left side

LEFT The early layout of the transmission compartment LHS, showing the straight-through design of the two ME exhaust pipes. In later vehicles, an expansion box was fitted over the gearbox.

BELOW Prototype undergoing mobility testing: ballast has been added to the nose to increase the weight up to 49.5 tons in order to replicate full stowage and ammunition. *(Courtesy Brian Clark)*

BELOW AND RIGHT G2 and P2: G2 was eventually sold to Germany in 1966, and has had the NBC pack added as well as the new suspension. P2 displays the original short hull configuration, with the very different rear, and the original suspension, wheels and tracks; she is also fitted with a trial Windsor turret. *(Courtesy M.P. Robinson and Brian Clark)*

ABOVE W4: a mock stowage box was bolted over the nose of the cast glacis, with a canvas cover over the turret front during early demonstrations, in order to keep the revolutionary shapes a secret for as long as possible. W4 put on a lot of mileage quickly and shows the signs of a hard life.

(Courtesy M.P. Robinson)

BELOW Four of the prototypes, in various different stages of modification, lined up for the Exercise PALLOS demonstration at Kirkcudbright in July 1963.

until November that year, and the many faults identified in the development trials led to the export falling further and further behind schedule; two production vehicles were eventually delivered in January 1966. In a reciprocal arrangement, two German Standard Panzers, later better known as Leopard, were sold to the UK, costing a much cheaper £350K for both.

Production

The next contract was for Leeds to build one pre-production tank (PP1), which was the first to be built with the new turret and glacis castings and extended rear hull with new suspension. This was generally similar to the Mk 1, and mounted a No 11 cupola, a twin jerrycan holder on the turret side, the No 2 NBC pack, and the Generating Unit Engine (GUE) exhaust on the rear face of the exhaust box. The first real order was placed on 10 October 1963 for 571 Chieftains; 39 were Mk 1 tanks, the order being split between ROFL (26) and Vickers (13). These tanks were for use in the UK only, in order to assist with further development and crew training.

The same contract also ordered 532 Mk 2s, with the production again divided on a 2:1 ratio between ROFL (355) and VA at Elswick (177), as well as £17 million of ammunition.[4] Chieftain was being thought of by some at this point as a stop-gap tank, and a part-buy seemed prudent; only seven out of the ten tank regiments in Germany, and none of the three in the UK, were to be equipped.[5] Producing all the tanks at Leeds would have been the cheaper option, but the government wanted the private VA tank production facility at Elswick to remain

4 In May 1960 the army had stated a requirement for 660 tanks, but this had been pared back for financial reasons.

5 It might be reasonable to question why sufficient Chieftains were not ordered simply to replace all the Centurions in use. The answer is in many ways a parallel with the later introduction of Challenger 1 to replace Chieftain: there was uncertainty – and some degree of hope – that a collaborative NATO tank might be a possibility, so rather than replace the whole fleet a part-buy seemed to be a good option.

LEFT Testing the tanks involved all sorts of theoretical and practical tests, including the inclinometer at the Longcross test track, shown here in use with a later service tank.

(Courtesy Brian Clark)

operational, as without the Chieftain order it may have had to close. Bad unemployment in the North-East, plus speed of production, turned out to be overriding political considerations: in 1962 a production estimate had revealed that ROFL could produce vehicles at a basic price of £38K each, and Vickers their vehicles at £44.25K each. At that stage the government clearly thought the extra £1.5 million a price worth paying to keep Elswick in business. The Treasury as always held the real power, and restricted in-year spending to allow an annual production of 200 tanks at 2:1, rather than the 300 per year requested by the Army Council.

Of the total, 353 of the Mk 2s would equip tank regiments in the British Army of the Rhine (BAOR). Also in Germany would be a war reserve of 76, plus another 46 in the repair pool; only 57 Mk 2s would remain in the UK. All vehicles destined for service in Germany had to incorporate what was termed the 'BAOR Standard', a whole series of essential modifications that had to be embodied to ensure that they were at the latest possible standard for front-line service. Production of the first bulk order started in 1965, with the first Mk 1 tank, 02EB13, being completed in June 1965 at Leeds, and the first Vickers Mk 1, 00EB23, in February 1966. By this time the army had confirmed that it was going to equip all its tank units with Chieftains: the requirement stated in 1966 was for a total of 1,013 MBTs, so, in effect, it was asking for another 442 to be built. The first Mk 2s came off the line in April 1966 and January 1967 from Leeds and Elswick respectively. Ninety-six Chieftain Mk 2 tanks had been built by the end of 1966, with

ABOVE LEFT A Hancolium flame-cutting machine, used to accurately cut the required shape in flat armour plates.

ABOVE The Universal Welding Manipulator, used to place the turret in the correct position and angle to facilitate gravity welding.

the total at 135 by April 1967; by the end of that year BAOR were holding 143 of them. By the end of April 1968, over 300 Mk 2s had been made.

Equipping ROFL for the Chieftain order had come at a price: in 1963, £980K was spent on plant, and another £450K on materials. The Treasury were understandably keen that this expenditure should be used beyond the initial contract for Mk 2 vehicles, and thus, when the next order (for the Mk 3) was being discussed, Leeds already had something of an advantage.

BELOW PP1 was extensively used for publicity and advertising: although never labelled as such, this tank was, in effect, the first Mk 1.

CHIEFTAIN

Chieftain : now in service

BATTLE TANK OF THE 1970's!

The fact that Leeds could also make the tanks quicker and 24% cheaper (by 1966, £41K each compared to Vickers' £54K) added to the commercial imperative, so despite protestations and pleadings from Vickers and a host of politicians, due to Treasury pressure the Mk 3 order placed on 27 February 1967 – and all subsequent orders for MBTs – went to Leeds. Other top-up orders for MBTs followed, and the last order for 45 Mk 5s was placed in 1971, bringing the total made for the British Army to 926 (Mk 1–Mk 5).

On 23 October 1970 – coincidentally the 28th anniversary of the Battle of El Alamein – it was stated that the army possessed 829 Chieftains that required a whole series of modifications to bring them up to the Mk 5 standard; this involved considerable and commendable foresight, as the Mk 5

itself would not start to appear for another 17 months. Included in this number were the Mk 1 tanks. But it was a huge undertaking, particularly as, by then, there were five marks of service tanks involved, with many different modification states on individual tanks. In June 1976, the MoD noted that it had 913 Chieftains in service; 97 of these were Mk 5s, with the remainder being fed into the Totem Pole programme. The object of Totem Pole was to bring all tanks from Mk 2 to 3/3 up to Mk 5 standard, by implementing all the myriad modifications needed – no small undertaking. The 39 Mk 1s were only to be used for driver training in the UK, and so only automotive modifications were carried out on them. Totem Pole was originally conceived as being a three-stage programme: stage X (fire-control modifications) would be implemented within

BRITISH ARMY PRODUCTION MARKS

Mk	Automotive	Turret and firepower	Equipment code	Remarks
1	Mk 4A 585bhp L60 engine. H30 Mk 7A GUE; two headlamps; no splashplate; ribbed trackguards	No 11 cupola; L11A1 120mm gun; M85 .50 RG; M73 Coax .30 MG; no Comd's MG; No 7 MBSGD	0300-2010	Majority converted to 1/1 or 1/2, and subsequently to 1/3 or 1/4. Engine later uprated to 650bhp.
2	Improved louvres; GUE exhaust moved to RHS of exhaust box; splashplate	No 15 Mk 1 cupola with L8 GPMG; L11A2 gun; Comd's L8 GPMG; No 9 MBSGD	0300-2020	Later fitted with Mk 6A 650bhp L60 engine. When Totem Pole modifications complete becomes Mk 6.
3	Mk 5A 650bhp L60 engine; H30 Mk 10A GUE; 12:1 parking brake; oil-lubricated axle arms and top rollers; four small headlamps and small splashplate; plain trackguards; simplified rear bins	No 15 Mk 2 cupola with angled periscopes and Comd's L37 GPMG; provision for TLS mounting; BML on gun; turret crew grips	0300-2030	When Totem Pole modifications complete becomes Mk 7.
3/G	As Mk 3 plus prototype turret/hull breathing		0300-2035	AKA 3(G). When Totem Pole modifications complete becomes Mk 7.
3/2	As Mk 3/G plus: ME cut-out switch	Prototype TLS mounting; Comd's firing handle	0300-2032	When Totem Pole modifications complete becomes Mk 7.
3/S	As Mk 3/G plus: Mk 6A 650bhp L60 engine; production turret/hull breathing; ME cut-out switch; electrical improvements	Comd's firing handle; new gunner's elevation handwheel; anchor block for HESH extraction tool	0300-2036	AKA 3(S). When Totem Pole modifications complete becomes Mk 7.
3/3	As Mk 3/S plus: Mk 7A 720bhp L60 engine; production turret/hull breathing; fuel tank isolation valve	Production TLS mounting; No 6 Mk 1 NBC pack; improved GCE metadynes in separate compartment; extended range graticule gunner's sight	0300-2033	When Totem Pole modifications complete becomes Mk 8.
5	As Mk 3/3 plus: uprated TN12 gearbox; low-loss exhaust; generator air cleaning filters; battery lagging and heating	L11A3 gun. Stage V charge bins; modified stowage; extended range graticule in gunner's telescope and Comd's sight; new thermal sleeve and gun clamp; reduced RG ammunition; increased APDS; Comd's MG elevation to 90°; plunger on VTL; No 6 Mk 2 NBC pack	0300-2050	The /4 suffix indicates sight modifications for APFSDS ammunition (also on Mks 6, 7 and 8). (Mk 5/2 in British service was to be Chieftain Mk 5 with appliqué Burlington (Chobham) armour packs.)

units, whilst the Y (automotive) changes could be done in a field workshop, and the Z (also automotive) had to be completed in a base workshop. In the event, the sheer quantity of tanks and the varied standards of them led to a specific Totem Pole line being established, so in a lot of cases X, Y and Z were implemented more or less concurrently in base workshops.

The introduction of Chieftain into Germany solved one problem for the army, in allowing the remaining Conquerors to be 'wasted out', and the termination of expensive spares contracts for them; the last was retired at the end of 1966. There was now no need to have a specialist long-distance 'hole puncher' in the tank regiments, they now had a true multi-role MBT. Interestingly, from the first order, 24 of the tanks were expected to be assigned as Observation Post (OP) tanks for Forward Operating Officers (FOOs) from two of the newly equipped Abbot regiments of the Royal Artillery (RA); it is not clear how these tanks would differ in configuration from standard gun tanks, but in the event none were ever used in this way. In 1967, a proposal was made to buy a further 771 tanks: this would equip another nine regiments, the Berlin Armoured Squadron, plus … the OP tanks in the RA Close Support regiments. This issue had clearly not yet gone away, and navigation equipment for the officers was still being discussed the following year, and revisited in 1972. (It never happened: FOOs never did operate Chieftain.)

Staggering though it is to relate, a project manager (PM) for Chieftain was not appointed until the end of 1968. Until then the work needed on all the various technical aspects of the tank was split between any number of government and military agencies, as well as ROFL. This clearly was organisationally poor, leading to wasted time and money, work being done in two or more places concurrently, or not being done at all. Bureaucratically it was a nightmare. Thankfully at last someone came to their senses and a PM (Lt Col Warren Piper) was appointed two years after the tank entered service, with a team of specialists, both civilian and military, to assist him, and finally something approaching coherence was brought to the programme.

Cost

Tanks cost a lot of money, and similar to the manner in which its weight increased, Chieftain became more and more expensive over the years. As our start point, Centurions, in March 1959, were estimated to cost £38K each. *Cost* here means the total of the expenses accrued in making one tank, whereas *price* refers to the amount of money required by a customer to purchase one tank (excluding ammunition, spares and any bespoke modifications). In 1960 – before production – it was estimated that one Chieftain was going to cost £56K; by 1962 this had risen to £67K, and only one year later to £94K. This large jump was due to the full development costs, including machinery, tooling and so on being factored in for the first time, and which more accurately reflected reality. In order to make a profit, it was decided in October 1963, that export versions should be priced at £115K, excluding radios and IR equipment. By 1968, Chieftains were costing around £84K each, excluding tools – costs come down as production increases, as the development and other costs are spread over a larger number of vehicles, including those built for export. The total cost of the development of the tank to that point was estimated at around £20 million, one-third of which was post-production development, a comment not only on the many problems caused by the engine and transmission, but also the many improvements and enhancements that new (and expensive) technology made possible – and which will be discussed at length later.

BRITISH ARMY VEHICLE PRODUCTION BY MAKER AND CONTRACT

Maker	Contract	Mark	Registrations	Total	Dates	Remarks
VA	KL/A/0208	1	00EB23–00EB35	13	Mar 66–Jan 67	£48,021 each.
	KL/A/0208	2	00EB36–02EB12	177	Jan 67–Sep 70	First 12 at £44,233 each, remainder £41,710 each.
ROFL	KL/A/0217	1	02EB13–02EB38	26	Jun 65–Mar 66	
	KL/A/0217	2	02EB39–05EB93	355	Apr 66–Aug 69	
	FVP/44/67	3	05FA84–07FA17	134	Sep 69–Jan 71	
	FVP/44/67		00FC51–00FC68	18	Dec 69–May 70	
	FVP/102/68	3/3	00FC04–00FC50	47	Jun 71–c.Feb 72	Dates estimated as cards missing: 00FC30 was built Oct 71.
	FVP/37/70		00FD01–00FD28	28	Oct 71–Mar 72	00FD01 and 02 built under Contract FVP/102/68.
	FVP/44/67	3/S	01FD00–01FD39	40	Jan 71–May 71	
	FVP/44/67	3/G	01FD40–01FD45	6	21–29 Oct 69	
	FVP/44/67	5	00FD54–00FD99	46	Mar 72–Jul 72	
	FVP/37/70		08FD51–08FD56	6	Jul 72–Aug 72	
	FVP/14/71		11FD32–11FD76	45	Jul 72–Apr 73	Final MBT 11FD76 completed 19 Apr 73.
	BP 059/017/202	AVLB Mk 2	00FB01–00FB04	4	Nov 68	Known as P1–P4. Eqpt code 0422-2021.
	FVP/83/69	AVLB Mk 5	01FD46–01FD82	37	Jun 73–Mar 77	Eqpt code 0422-2050 and 3000.
	FV15998	ARV Mk 5	06FF78–07FF52	75	Jul 75–May 77	Many converted to ARRV. Eqpt code 0505-2050 (ARRV Mk 7 0505-3003).
	FV15998		00GC01–00GC11	11	May–Dec 77	
	N/K	ARV Training	00HB81–00HB83	3	Aug–Dec 80	Converted from 03SP18 (ARV), 20 and 21 (AEV(W)).

Source: Tank Museum, Bovington, record cards.
Notes:
1 Some 29 cards are completely or partly missing, leading to occasional uncertainty in dates and registrations.
2 All tanks were capable of being converted to either Command or Control versions, although at least three tanks were built specifically as Command variants *ab initio*: 03EB32, 33 and 05EB40.

BRITISH ARMY VEHICLE PRODUCTION BY TYPE

Type and mark	Number built	Remarks
MBT prototypes	14	P1–6, W1–6, G1, G2.
MBT pre-production	1	PP1.
AEV(W)	2	E1, E2.
Sub-total development	**17**	
MBT Mk 1	39	UK training use only.
MBT Mk 2	532	
MBT Mk 3	152	
MBT Mk 3/3	75	
MBT Mk 3/S	40	
MBT Mk 3/G	6	
MBT Mk 5	97	
Sub-total MBT	**941**	
AVLB Mk 2	4	Effectively the prototypes for AVLB Mk 5.
AVLB Mk 5	37	Does not include 11 AVLB Mk 6 converted from Mk 1/4 gun tanks.
Sub-total AVLB	**41**	
ARV prototype	2	R1, R2, R3 cancelled before being built.
ARV Mk 5	86	Does not include 3 Training ARV converted from R1, E1 and E2.
Sub-total ARV	**88**	
Total all types	**1,087**	All AVRE were conversions from MBT chassis.

LEFT A rare image of a prototype in colour, showing the semi-gloss Deep Bronze Green colour then in vogue, and the khaki-green canvas cover hiding the shape of the turret front.

The final Mk 5 production tank for the British Army, 11FD76, entered service in mid-1973, having come off the Leeds production line on 19 April of that year, ending a production run for the British Army which only lasted about eight years. How can we best summarise the introduction of Chieftain into service? We must acknowledge that Chieftain was in some ways rushed into service, despite its many known faults, particularly with the engine and mobility. This was due to two overriding reasons, one military and one commercial. Firstly, there was an urgent need to offset the considerable numerical advantages possessed by Soviet armoured forces likely to be operating in northern Europe, and, secondly, Centurion production at both Leeds and Elswick was coming to an end and it was uneconomic to attempt to restart it. The tank was accepted for service – conditional 'on the remedying of many defects' on 1 May 1963. The remedying of defects proved to be a recurring theme throughout Chieftain's service history, with a multitude of modifications and new systems being fitted. As an example, during the three-year production run of Mk 2 tanks, no less than 1,480 changes were introduced to the tank.

In summary, we can see how the development history of Chieftain was anything but plain sailing, and begin to appreciate how problems in this area can have serious knock-on effects to the tank in the hands of its crews. We will now turn our attention to examining some of the details of the hull and turret, and then look at the tank in service, including the fascinating and little-understood history of attempts to sell the tank into overseas markets.

LEFT Three images from a very early user handbook showing the proposed external configuration of the Mk 1 – it shows the early Light Projector, smoke grenade dischargers, NBC pack and rear turret basket, and turret stowage bins, as well as no power take-off for the Dozer kit. Note also the position of the GUE exhaust, and that the main engine exhausts are facing upwards.

RIGHT The shape of things to come – unfortunately! A very early L60 engine being changed on W5 during the FV434 trials in 1964.

Chapter Two

Hull and mobility

Chieftain was designed to be a simple tank to drive, which it was. However, in many other regards it was complex and thus difficult and time-consuming to maintain. In particular, it was let down by the failure to make the L60 engine both reliable and powerful, a problem which took two decades to resolve and which stained the reputation of the tank both during its service and through the prism of history.

OPPOSITE Dust! Sgt Tony Stirling 17/21L kicks up lots of it in Canada in 1990. Filtering it out to prevent it wrecking the engine was a headache for the designers, and meant repetitive preventative maintenance for the crews.

ABOVE Strategic mobility could only be achieved using ships, as the tank was too large and heavy to be flown. *(Courtesy Andrew Chapman)*

BELOW Operational mobility. The most common method of moving tanks long distances was – and is – by rail flats. Notice the method of cross-shackling the tanks down, and also how the tracks overhang the sides.

Mobility

In British doctrine, there are three types of mobility. Strategic mobility involves moving long distances, from the normal home base to a new theatre of operations, whether for training or for war. As Chieftain was too large and heavy for the aircraft operated by the RAF, the only method of achieving strategic mobility was by sea, using either ships of the Royal Fleet Auxiliary, or civil ships hired for the purpose. Rotating the fleet of tanks to and from the training establishment in Canada was, of course, conducted using this method. Next, operational mobility is the movement within the theatre of operations over distances beyond that which the vehicle can sensibly move under its own power. Typically, there are two main ways of achieving this – by tank transporter and by rail. Both were used extensively by the British Army, and Chieftain crews became adept at both types of transportation. (Or should one say 'mostly adept', as the accompanying photographs indicate that this was not always so.)

Finally, we have tactical mobility, the movement of Chieftain on its own tracks, either by road or cross-country. For speed and comfort, not to mention fuel economy and reduced breakdowns, wherever possible road movement would be the preferred option, but that option could not generally be taken when occupying fire positions, and so cross-country movement was then the norm. Chieftain crews based in BAOR learned their craft on the wasteland of the SLTA between Hamburg and Hannover, an area badly mauled by generations of tank training. There was an advantage to this, as drivers became skilled at operating in really poor terrain, which meant that they were very well trained in route selection and crossing obstacles. When operating in the

LEFT Operational mobility by tank transporter. Great care had to be taken to ensure that the tank was square-on before this point, as the driver lost sight of the guide and all he could see for a few seconds at the point of balance was the sky, before the nose dipped on to the trailer bed. *(Courtesy Andrew Chapman)*

ABOVE Not the fault of the tank driver. This tank transporter managed to roll off the road in 1981, losing its load and presenting the REME with an interesting triple recovery challenge.

BELOW Tactical mobility. Rafting exercises on the River Havel in Berlin. The German-built M2 rigs used by the RE could be used as a raft or joined together to form a pontoon bridge.

much better terrain conditions of German farmland on a Field Training Exercise (FTX), it all became rather plain sailing. Or should one say, once again, 'mostly', as accidents could and did happen. Chieftain, despite its high weight and poor engine power, could be driven relatively fast across all types of cross-country terrain, and its Horstmann suspension allowed maximum use to be made of the available power. Although the overall tactical mobility of it cannot be compared in any way with its

RIGHT Tactical mobility. Driving across country at speed, kicking up mud and leaving a cloud of tell-tale white smoke behind.

ABOVE Chieftain was designed to ford up to 1.07m unprepared but the ground underneath had to be solid enough not to get bogged. A Sqn 3RTR on the SLTA in 1985. *(Courtesy Andy Fisher)*

ABOVE RIGHT Mk 2 04EB42, having driven off the side of an unseen concrete obstacle on the Hohne range complex. The yellow range flag is correctly used, as it indicates 'I have a mechanical problem'! *(Courtesy Andy Fisher)*

successor, Challenger, for its time it was a good tank – when it was not broken down, of course, more of which presently.

Armoured obesity

Before investigating the tactical mobility aspects of Chieftain, including how to drive it, we will now look at a problem Chieftain faced throughout its life, which was how to keep its weight down – increased weight, of course, puts more strain on components, as well as reducing the critical power-to-weight ratio.[6] We might recall that the original intention was for Chieftain to weigh no more than 45 tons. This, of course, was based upon the original characteristics defined in 1954 as:

- V8 engine (no multi-fuel requirement) in a hull length of 22ft 3in;
- 105mm bag-charge gun;
- Lightweight Ranging Gun (RG) and Machine Guns (MGs);
- Steel tracks;

- Centurion-type suspension and 28in roadwheels;
- Frontal immunity at 700yd (640m) from Soviet 100mm gun-firing Armour-Piercing High Explosive (APHE);
- 60 rounds of MA ammunition;
- Gun elevation +15°, depression –7°.

By 1958 the tank was estimated as weighing in at 50.3 tons, and by late 1962, in reality, was up to 52.7 tons, fully crewed and stowed.[7] How did this come about – and what could be done about it? The answer to the first question can largely be answered in one word: development. As the tank was built, trialled and modified, a range of essential modifications remorselessly added weight. These were:

- Adoption of L60 multi-fuel engine and associated increase in length of hull;
- Subsequent L60 modifications including larger oil tank, cooling fans and radiators, plus dampers;
- Revised engine decks and exhaust systems;
- Gun calibre increased to 120mm;
- Rubber track pads (which could be removed on mobilisation if time allowed);
- Strengthened suspension and 31.6in roadwheels (leading to a longer run of track required);
- Increased frontal armour to provide immunity from expected Soviet gun/ammunition;

---

6 Chieftain, even with the 750bhp engine fitted, only reached 14.6bhp per ton. M60 was 15.6, T55 was 16 and Leopard about 22.

7 A full load of fuel and ammunition added well over 2 tons; even the four-man crew without personal effects and stowage added one-third of a ton.

- Water-filled charge bin containers;
- Gun elevation increased to +20°, depression –10°;
- Armoured searchlight;
- Tow bar.

The lengthened hull for the new version of the L60 added about 1 ton. Just putting rubber pads on to a redesigned track (in order to meet German requirements for driving on roads) added just over, and the new suspension and roadwheels just under, another ton. The height increase needed to allow the increased range of gun elevation added an unspecified but certainly considerable amount of weight. The pressurised water/coolant mix in the charge bin containers added both survivability and another 360lb. Furthermore, though this was probably an exaggeration, one official report spoke of a typical tank in the field carrying up to 2 tons of mud in its suspension, and, of course, once in service the crew tended to add additional stowage to make the tank more habitable and efficient. It was a rare tank that did not have at least two additional bins added on to the rear of the turret baskets, as well as carrying liberal amounts of oils and lubricants to allow frequent topping up. Additionally, other systems reached maturity and were added to the tank in order to enhance its capability, but again at the cost of increasing weight still further. Amongst these were:

- Revised stowage including turret baskets;
- Turret breathing;
- Increased APDS stowage (six extra bag-charge containers);
- No 2 NBC pack and trunking (later replaced by the even heavier No 6);
- IR and Radiation Detection (RADIAC) equipment;
- Tank Laser Sight (TLS) and Muzzle Reference System (MRS) (compensated for to some degree by removal of RG);
- Improved Fire Control System (IFCS);
- Stillbrew armour;
- Thermal Observation and Gunnery Sight (TOGS).

These added significant weight to Chieftain. For example, Stillbrew added 2.25 tons; the No 2 NBC pack over half a ton, and even the

ABOVE Mud! Chieftain's suspension could pick up enormous amounts of the glutinous sticky stuff, which added to the weight and had to be cleaned away before servicing or repairs. Sgt Bob Jacobs and LCpl Paddy Coombe contemplate the task ahead with undisguised enthusiasm.

revised stowage came with a 1,200lb weight penalty. The tanks were also fitted with steel plates, known as bazooka plates by the crews, to protect the suspension units from damage in combat. At 6mm thick, these added significant weight to an already overloaded tank. In order to remove some of this weight, 0.75in aluminium versions were introduced around the late 1970s; these were very popular with the

BELOW The main glacis casting was a heavy and intricate piece of work. It was substantially redesigned to the configuration shown here in 1964 in order to save weight.

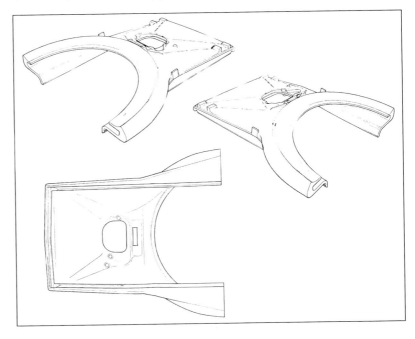

ABOVE LEFT The front casting for the hull, showing the slight angle introduced to the centreline, in order to increase the driver's legroom.

ABOVE Fitting the new style of turret with a reduced angle of maximum armour coverage – although not thickness – during production.

LEFT W4 showing off the original – and very heavy – tow bar fitted to the prototypes. The need to remove all surplus weight led to it being deleted on service tanks.

BELOW In service in its heaviest form as a Mk 11 with Stillbrew and TOGS, this is the Royal Scots Dragoon Guards (Scots DG) on exercise – note the improvised canvas covers over the headlamps.

crews, as one man could handle them on his own, whereas the steel versions always took two people to remove and replace.[8] From all this it can be appreciated that the dream of a 45-ton tank was just that. It was clear that one of the major reasons for the many problems with the L60 engine and the TN12 gearbox was that they were being used in a tank weighing about 17% more than they were designed for. (The reader might wish to consider the effects on *their* mobility if they weighed that amount more than they currently do.) The real question, though, and one which was constantly being asked, was what could be done about it?

In December 1962, a study concluded that there were a number of ways in which weight could be taken off. Removing the 17mm armour from the searchlight would save about 1,250lb,

8   Aluminium bazooka plates could be identified easily as they had square-section lashing eyes, rather than the round ones on the steel versions.

and the removal of the requirement for the tank to swim using rigid panel equipment about 600lb. Reducing the MA ammunition load by six HESH and three charge bin containers would save another 350lb – but by then it was realised that the law of diminishing returns applied. The only way that another substantial saving could be made was by reducing the amount of armour carried. With a heavy heart (pun intended) this was done, as in the final analysis it came down to priorities: was more protection or less weight the critical factor? It was decided in early 1964 to reduce the angle of armour protection – but not the thickness – afforded by the turret and glacis castings from 60° to 45°, and the tank was redesigned substantially as a result, with PP1, the pre-production model, the first to show the new shape. Around one-third of a ton was removed by doing this. At the same time, it was decided that the driver needed slightly more legroom along the centreline for his feet when closed down. The front of the hull was modified by making the noseplate slightly angled rather than straight, with the glacis casting modified to match, adding back some of the savings. The floor plates under the hull were built in a shallow V rather than flat; this also added some weight but was not done, as is commonly thought, to increase mine resistance (the V was much too shallow to add any meaningful protection), but rather to make the hull less likely to stick in deep mud, thereby enhancing mobility.

Driving Chieftain

In broad terms, Chieftain followed a conventional layout, common to many British post-war tanks: a four-man crew, with the driver in the hull, and the three other crewmen in the turret. The loader/radio operator occupied the left-hand side (LHS) of the turret, with the commander on the right, and the gunner forward and below him. The breech of the MA took up the majority of the space in the front centre of the turret, with ammunition stowage in the form of projectile racks in the turret and hull, including in the driver's cab, with pressurised charge bin containers for the bag-charges below the turret ring in the hull. The Main Engine (ME), GUE and gearbox occupied the rear of the hull, with final drives and sprockets

ABOVE More weight. A Chieftain Mk 10 with additional stowage bins and SIMFICS as well as Stillbrew negotiates the mud. *(TM 3627A4)*

at the rear. The suspension on each side comprised three twin roadwheel and top roller Horstmann units, bolted to the hull, with a front track-adjusting idler wheel. However, Chieftain also incorporated a number of revolutionary design features, of which the most important ones relating to the hull and mobility were:

■ The centrally located reclining driver.
■ The semi-automatic gearbox.

We will now investigate these two aspects in more detail, and in so doing, learn how to start up and drive the beast.

In order to reduce height and thus weight, it was decided to place the driver on the centreline of the hull. This was possible as there was no longer a requirement for tanks to have five-man crews, with a co-driver/hull machine gunner having to be accommodated in the hull alongside the driver. Putting the driver in the centre conferred a number of advantages: the control cables, hydraulic lines and electrical cables could all be routed along the centreline of the hull to the rear; additional ammunition could be stowed either side of him; when closed down he found it much easier to judge the width of the tank, important when crossing bridges or negotiating minefield gaps; and he could exit, in an emergency, through the turret. Protecting the driver was a single-piece armoured hatch, which was operated from inside the cab and which rose and then swung to the right on a sprung pillar before being locked in the open (head-out) position. The driver's view when closed down was through a No 36 periscope,

CHIEFTAIN MBT – MAIN FEATURES. *(Josh Hodgson)*

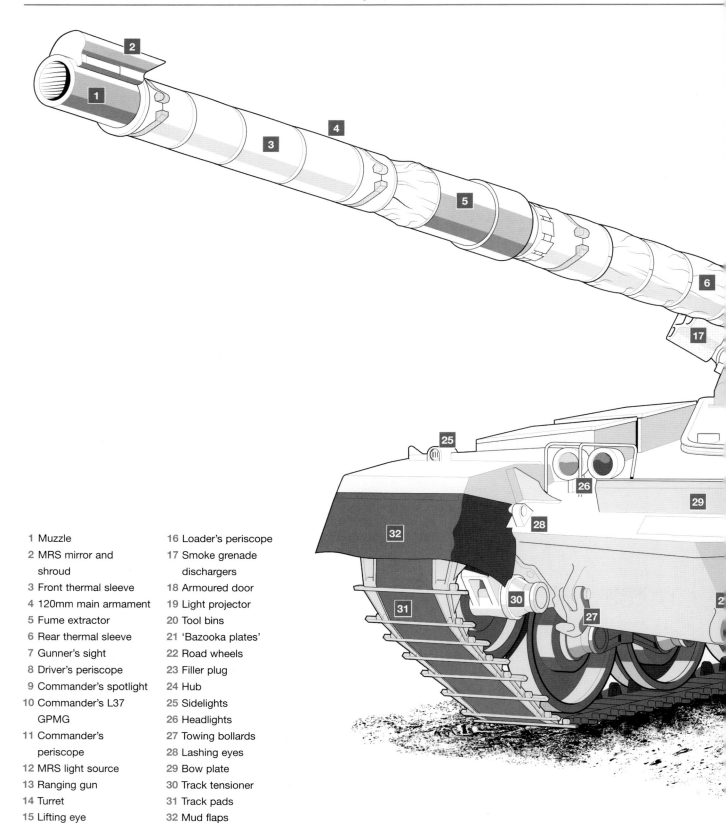

1 Muzzle	16 Loader's periscope
2 MRS mirror and shroud	17 Smoke grenade dischargers
3 Front thermal sleeve	18 Armoured door
4 120mm main armament	19 Light projector
5 Fume extractor	20 Tool bins
6 Rear thermal sleeve	21 'Bazooka plates'
7 Gunner's sight	22 Road wheels
8 Driver's periscope	23 Filler plug
9 Commander's spotlight	24 Hub
10 Commander's L37 GPMG	25 Sidelights
11 Commander's periscope	26 Headlights
12 MRS light source	27 Towing bollards
13 Ranging gun	28 Lashing eyes
14 Turret	29 Bow plate
15 Lifting eye	30 Track tensioner
	31 Track pads
	32 Mud flaps

which could be replaced for night-time use by an IR (later II) night periscope. The seat was a clever and comfortable design, well padded and adjustable. For driving head out with the hatch open, two levers either side of the seat were operated to place it in an upright 'armchair position'. Operating the same two levers could also drop the seat back rearwards until the driver was near-horizontal. In order to drive in this reclined or 'supine' position using his periscope, he would raise the two steering tillers (generally referred to as the 'sticks') into the upright position so that he could reach them easily, and then adjust the headrest of the seat until he could see through the periscope window.

ABOVE AND RIGHT
Driving head out …

FAR RIGHT … and in the closed-down position using the seat headrest to look through the No 36 periscope. *(Courtesy David Moffat)*

RIGHT Inside the driver's cab. The seat is in the reclined position, but the two steering tillers, aka sticks, are in the forward position, used when driving head out.

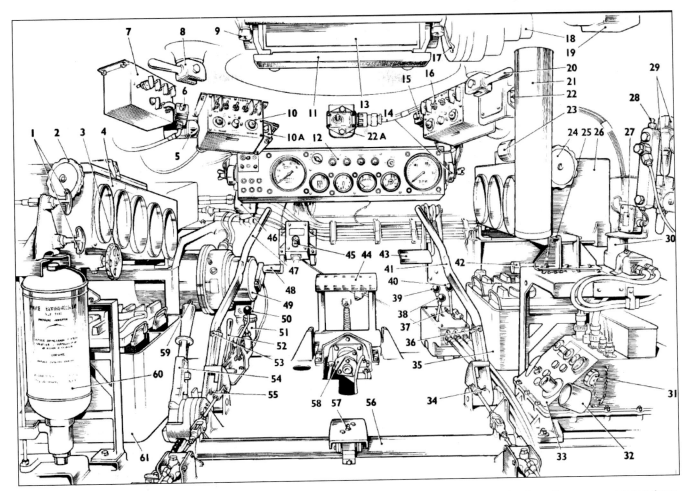

1	Fixed fire extinguisher operating handles	32	Inter-vehicle starting socket cover
2	Projectile locking handle	33	Driver's master switchbox
3	Rack lifting jack operating handle	34	Steering lever lubricator
4	Projectile rack	35	Right battery box
5	Fire alarm warning light	36	Right steering lever locating pawl catch
6	Reverse button	37	Emergency gear lever locking plate
7	Lights switchboard	38	Generating unit engine governor control
8	Driver's access door locking handle (left)		lever (H30 Mk 7A engine vehicles)
9	Driver's periscope mounting knurled nut	39	Generating unit engine fuel cut-off lever
10	Generating unit engine switchboard	40	Emergency gear control lever
10A	Dust extractor warning light, all marks except Mk 1	41	Right steering lever
11	Driver's periscope swing bar	42	Rack lifting jack
12	Driver's instrument panel	43	Accelerator pedal
13	Driver's periscope	44	Brake pedal
14	Driver's instrument panel mounting	45	Driving lights dipswitch
15	Horn button	46	Negative line junction box
16	Main engine switchboard	47	Left steering lever
17	Periscope wiper parking lever	48	Gearbox controller pedal
18	Periscope wiper motor	49	Gearbox controller
19	Radio distribution box	50	Hydraulic starter pinion control lever
20	Driver's access door locking handle (right)	51	Hydraulic starter master cylinder and
21	Driver's access door spring tube		reservoir (H30 Mk 7A engine vehicles)
22	Driver's safety switch (early vehicles)	52	Hydraulic starter pump clutch lever
22A	Driver's safety switch (later vehicles)	53	Left steering lever location pawl catch
23	Fire extinguisher	54	Parking brake lever
24	Projectile locking handle	55	Steering lever lubricator
25	Rack retaining pin	56	Steering mechanism cross-shaft
26	Projectile rack	57	Steering interlock lubricating nipple
27	Battery thermal switch junction box	58	Brake power valve
28	Bleed nipple	59	Release button (parking brake lever
29	Main brake warning light pressure switches		retaining pawl)
30	Dozer equipment	60	Fixed fire extinguishers
31	Inspection light socket cover	61	Left battery box

Starting the ME could be done by one of two ways. The recommended method was to start the GUE first, as this took a lot less battery power to get going, and then use the hydraulic start system to get the ME running off the GUE without using the electric starter motor. However, crewmen are only human and therefore lazy, and most preferred to start the ME using the much simpler electric start method, which took more battery power and therefore ran the risk of draining the batteries, which would then require a 'slave start' from another tank. To start the tank electrically, carry out a full first parade, and then make sure that the handbrake is fully on (54) and the emergency gear lever (40) is in neutral. Now switch on the master switch (33), which controls power from the four hull batteries. Switch on (down) switches 2, 3 and 4 on the ME switchboard (16) and then press the starter button on the same box for a few seconds. The engine will start – if it does not start readily after two or three attempts do not continue

as the batteries will be rapidly discharged; instead, use the hydraulic start method. Once the engine has started, switch on switch 5 on the ME switchboard (16) which will bring the ME generator on line, allowing many of the heavy load facilities to be used – GCE, Light Projector, NBC pack and so on. The batteries will also be recharged.

For such a large and heavy tank, Chieftain was actually fairly easy to drive, as the decision to use a semi-automatic gearbox took away a lot of the hard labour associated with manual gear changes, and with six forward gears, gear changing was a frequent occurrence. With the engine started, we are ready to move off. Place both feet firmly on the footbrake (44) and release the handbrake (54) – gears cannot be selected with the handbrake on. Transfer the left foot to the Gearbox Controller Pedal (GCP) (48) and kick it up once to select first gear – the gear selected will be shown on the instrument panel (12). Place the left foot back on the footbrake, and then put the right foot on the accelerator pedal (43). Accelerate slowly and smoothly at the same time as releasing pressure on the footbrake, changing up at about 1,800rpm, either by using the tachometer on the instrument panel, or, with experience, by listening to the note of the engine. Gear changing to a higher gear is done by kicking up the GCP, and changing down by kicking down, very similar to a motorcycle gear change. However, when changing gear on Chieftain, a technique called 'duck feet' is employed. This involves flicking both feet up when changing up, in order to briefly let off on the engine revs at the same time that the change is made, and flicking both feet down when changing down, in order to 'blip' the accelerator and give a burst of revs. This will make for a much smoother gear change.

Be aware that a gearbox governor is fitted, which will prevent a down-change if the revs are too high. The main reason it is fitted, however, is to slow the tank down if the main brake accumulator pressure fails, by changing down through the gears; the governor automatically changes down once the revs drop to 800, and was meant to complete a down-change every 1.6 seconds until the tank was in first gear. It could be – and often was – disconnected by the crew, to give the driver more control, at the expense of less safety. (The commander is also provided with an emergency stop switch in his position to shut off the ME in an emergency.) The most difficult technique for a new driver to learn is how to change down smoothly: there is a big gap in ratios between fourth and third, and changing down at the wrong revs will cause the tank to brake momentarily, accompanied by both a violent dip of the nose and much cursing from the rest of the crew.

Steering is simple, if sometimes requiring more than a little muscle power – this is made easier if the tracks are kept at the right tension, the hydraulics have been bled and the steering brake pads are in good condition. In essence, keep the revs high prior to steering by changing down as necessary, and pull the stick corresponding to the direction of the turn, increasing throttle as required. Change down whilst turning if the revs drop too low. Once the tank is pointing in the desired direction, release the pressure on the stick and the tank will move in a straight line once more. Slight pressure on the stick will provide fine adjustment to the direction when necessary, and quickly flicking the stick is often all that is required. It can be seen that, although the Chieftain was in many ways a complicated tank, in other ways it was designed to be as simple as possible, but it should be realised that although driving was a fairly straightforward operation – as we will hear later, it was claimed that a child could do it – the maintenance that accompanied the role was mostly heavy, dirty and repetitive.

BELOW So simple that anyone could drive it? Actually, as the Duke of Edinburgh was a very experienced pilot, driving a Chieftain would be ridiculously easy.

The never-ending story – developing the L60 engine

There is no doubt that, in discussions on the merits and otherwise of the Chieftain, the L60 engine will feature prominently as the villain of the piece. It was always seen as the Achilles heel of the tank, and therefore an explanation is required as to why this was so. In 1988, Royal Armament Research & Development Establishment (RARDE) very helpfully produced a report entitled 'A development history of the L60 engine for Chieftain MBT'. This was a conscious decision to record the tempestuous history of Chieftain's power plant, even though it was stated that 'this design of engine is unlikely ever to be used again', just in case the story would prove to be of use to later engine designers; it certainly is of interest to us. The following history of the L60 relies very heavily on that document, largely authored by a Mr T. O'Callaghan, to whom we are all greatly indebted, as indeed we are for another excellent L60 development report produced by REME Major Iain McArthur of Military Vehicles and Engineering Establishment (MVEE).

Although the Chieftain can trace its origins back to 1950, the development of the L60 did not truly begin until 1959 – so why the long gap? In 1951, the specification for the Medium Tank No 2 aka FV4201 was being considered, and a key design factor was its weight, to be no more than 45 tons. In order to meet the mobility requirements of being 'at least as good as Centurion', a 700bhp engine was decided upon, which would have given about 15.5bhp per ton – the power-to-weight ratio. It was to be a diesel compression ignition (CI) type, as Centurion's thirsty petrol engine was that tank's major failing, and it was thought that the much better fuel consumption obtained with a diesel would offer logistic benefits. However, this was before the huge increase in the use of commercial diesel-engine vehicles. NATO planners had concerns that diesel might become scarce in wartime, and so it was decided in 1955 that NATO policy should be to use multi-fuel engines. This policy required that, as well as running on diesel, the following fuels should also be able to be used 'with little or no adjustment': gas turbine, gasoline (70–80

LEFT Why would they want to advertise who was responsible for it? Leyland struggled to make the L60 both powerful and reliable – the crews might have settled for just one or the other. (TM 10065.089)

octane petrol), premium-grade motor spirit or a mixture of these. Like so many NATO policies, it suited no one and all of the participating nations quietly ignored it … except Britain. British designers were told to meet the requirement, and this decision was at the heart of Chieftain's subsequent troubles, and led to its enduring reputation as an unreliable tank.

The competing size, power and fuel requirements meant that there was no readily available engine for the new tank, so one would have to be designed from scratch. Two companies were initially contracted in late 1955 to develop possible multi-fuel engines, Rover and Leyland. In January 1956, Rover were asked to build a spark-ignition engine, and Leyland to develop a CI alternative; both firms started by looking at V8 solutions. However, Rover then decided that they were not going to continue in the military engines market and withdrew in 1957. Leyland, meanwhile, realised that they could not get 700bhp out of the V8, and started work on a V12, the intention being to nestle the GUE between the two cylinder banks; however, the overall size proved to be just too large and the work was abandoned in early 1958, having cost the taxpayer £150K. A completely new engine design was urgently needed.

In 1954 the Rootes Group had introduced a novel supercharged diesel engine called the TS3. This was a 2-stroke 3-cylinder engine, with two horizontally opposed inward-facing pistons per cylinder. It developed only 90–120bhp, but was extremely advanced for the time. FVRDE had conducted trials on the TS3, and by 1957 had run one for several thousand miles with excellent results, and which crucially had shown that a 2-stroke opposed piston engine was the best

ABOVE Inside an early L60, before the viscous dampers were found to be necessary. *(Courtesy M.P. Robinson)*

BELOW Two early L60 powerpacks – with dampers – being used during the trials of the FV434 REME vehicle in 1964.

configuration for multi-fuel, having the additional advantage of being reasonably compact. Leyland was therefore directed to design a larger version of such an engine, designated L60 (which stood for Leyland Model 60). Because of their expertise Rootes were asked to assist Leyland, but the commercial negotiations then took a year to complete. The main features of the engine design were not agreed until May 1958, and the development contract was only issued three months later, so over two years were, in effect, wasted. Two myths can be well and truly busted at this point: whilst serving I was frequently told that one of the reasons that the Chieftain engine

was so poor was because it was a modified Leyland bus engine. It was not; it was designed specifically for the tank, but ruined during design because of the multi-fuel requirement specified by NATO. Secondly, the German Junkers Jumo aircraft engine of the Second World War is often noted as the basis of the L60. It was not. It may have helped in the development of the TS3 but was only indirectly involved in the design of the new much larger powerpack. (Interestingly, however, the Jumo was designed to be used either vertically opposed or, by turning it through 90°, horizontally opposed, an option which might have been considered for the L60 and which might have prevented some of the oil-related problems.)

The first L60 was, therefore, not built and tested until 1959, bearing in mind that six prototype tanks had already been ordered in April 1957, with the first one due to be completed in January 1960. The initial engine tests exposed a litany of problem areas – cooling, lubrication, oil filtration, fan drive unreliability, air cleaner and exhaust problems, excessive smoke, and oil and coolant leaks; it might have been quicker to list what worked well. It was decided that the engine needed to be substantially redesigned, with one of the modifications including the addition of a damping system to cure excessive torsional vibrations particularly at low revs; this led to a lengthened engine and thus a longer hull was needed on the tank … leading to an increase in weight by around a ton. Indeed, the dampers used were chosen because they added the least length and thus weight, and not necessarily because they were technically the best solution. It was also specified that, to allow for rapid field repairs, the engine had to be removable as a unit, complete with cooling and lubrication systems; this would facilitate test running as a complete unit. This was not quite the same as the modern concept of a powerpack, as the transmission (and indeed the GUE) was removed separately; in order to do this, the special flexible engine to transmission linkage known as the Twiflex coupling had to be unbolted.

When the first prototype tanks were trialled in BAOR in 1962 using Mk 2 engines, concerns were immediately expressed on the amount of white smoke produced, their general unreliability

and also a lack of power – it was clear that much more power was going to be needed to move Chieftain's increasing bulk around. One thing that mitigated this to some extent was the excellent ride delivered by the Horstmann suspension, which at least allowed all the available power to be utilised. But the multi-fuel requirement was the overriding design requirement for the L60. In order to achieve efficient combustion of all the fuel types, the combustion chamber needed to be as compact and as hot as possible, which caused endless problems when trying to run the engine on petrol. The design of the fuel injection system also had to be constantly revised to try to meet the requirements of all the possible fuels; it would have been very much quicker, easier and of course cheaper if the only fuel specified was diesel.

A report noted that, compared to Centurion's much-vaunted Meteor 'at the same stage of development', the L60 had demonstrated better reliability; this was naïve at best, and might be viewed as papering over the cracks. The L60

ABOVE LEFT AND ABOVE If only … Chieftain's engine had been designed around running on diesel fuel only, many of the subsequent problems could have been avoided.

BELOW LEFT AND BELOW Just how bad could the problem of white smoke be? This bad! To be fair, as the L60 was improved the amount of smoke decreased, but the lower image is probably as good as it got. *(Courtesy Meyrick Griffin-Jones and Keith Paget)*

requirement demanded that the average Mean Distance Between Failures (MDBF) should be 2,500 miles, equivalent to just over three years' normal service in BAOR and about double that expected from Centurion; it was not until the early 1980s that a figure approaching that – 2,200 miles MDBF – was achieved. The MGO Gen Sir Charles Richardson was nearer the mark when he said that '… in 1963 the army had a promising new tank with an unreliable engine. If work on the engine had started five years earlier, there would have been little or no need … to improve its reliability.' At the same time he confirmed that the 550bhp engines being used were not acceptable for service tanks, and that at least 700bhp had to be achieved. In an automotive report on the Mk 2 in 1968, the RAC were able to opine that 'The Chieftain is more reliable than the present Centurion' – damned by faint praise? Another report of the period stated that 'All users agree that Chieftain is a marked improvement over Centurion in all respects, but the euphoria created by the introduction of a new tank is over. There are several major operational deficiencies in Chieftain which users are discovering …' This discovery could be brutal. In July 1969, the newly formed Blues and Royals took their equally new Chieftains on to the SLTA for the first time. They suffered the almost total loss of their fleet, about forty Chieftains breaking down in ten days, leaving only three 'on the road'. Inexperience must have contributed, but so did the environment:

the weather was unusually dry and there were extremely high levels of dust, akin to desert conditions. The investigation that followed led to the development of a new air cleaner filter element and better sealing of the air cleaner to the engine. Crews were required to remove the filter regularly in dusty conditions and knock out as much dust as possible; this was known as 'banging out the biscuit' and became a regular sight. It helped to reduce the potential for dust ingress into the engine, where it would otherwise form a grinding paste with the oil and wreck the internal components.

The specific areas that caused the most problems in the L60 were: the cylinder liners, the pistons, fuel injection and combustion, the air cleaner, the exhaust system and the cooling system. It is worth having a look at each of these problem areas in a little detail. Cylinder liners are sleeves fitted into the cylinders that have to balance the need for mechanical strength with good wear characteristics; these two requirements are not complimentary and a benefit in one area normally adversely affects the other. The L60 suffered, as development work on finding the best liner should have been completed before the engine was ever fitted into the tank, but, as this was not to be, it had to be carried out whilst the tank was in service. There was no real alternative to trial and error, and over a dozen liner materials were trialled until it was decided to adopt Cast Iron 16 (CI-16) with a surface layer of Laystall silicon carbide. Additionally, the lip seals constantly cracked and failed, allowing coolant to leak into the exhaust and causing (some of) the white smoke. Lastly, the design of the inlet and exhaust ports was hugely problematic, and restricted the amount of power that each engine design could deliver; this was eventually addressed by changing the number of ports, and heavily modifying the exhaust and fuel systems. Once again, a major culprit was the multi-fuel requirement, which prevented the designers from optimising the engine for diesel only.

The pistons presented a similar story, with problems occurring that, once again, were related to the multi-fuel requirement. The official history lamented: 'As soon as one solution is reached a fault appears elsewhere.' Many of the early piston failures were related to crown

BELOW A REME Field Repair Team conduct a pack change on Salisbury Plain, 1977.

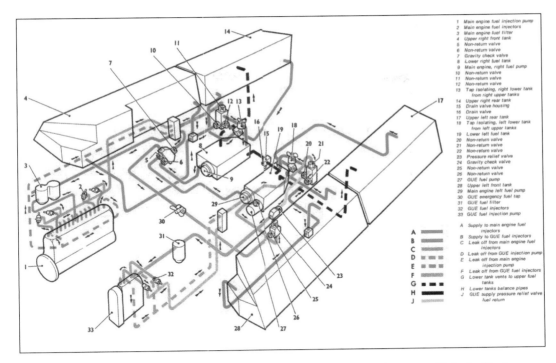

1	Main engine fuel injection pump
2	Main engine fuel injectors
3	Main engine fuel filter
4	Upper right front tank
5	Non-return valve
6	Non-return valve
7	Gravity check valve
8	Lower right fuel tank
9	Main engine, right fuel pump
10	Non-return valve
11	Non-return valve
12	Non-return valve
13	Tap isolating, right lower tank from right upper tanks
14	Upper right rear tank
15	Drain valve housing
16	Drain valve
17	Upper left rear tank
18	Tap isolating, left lower tank from left upper tanks
19	Lower left fuel tank
20	Non-return valve
21	Non-return valve
22	Non-return valve
23	Pressure relief valve
24	Gravity check valve
25	Non-return valve
26	Non-return valve
27	GUE fuel pump
28	Upper left front tank
29	Main engine left fuel pump
30	GUE emergency fuel tap
31	GUE fuel filter
32	GUE fuel injectors
33	GUE fuel injection pump

A	Supply to main engine fuel injectors
B	Supply to GUE fuel injectors
C	Leak off from main engine fuel injectors
D	Leak off from GUE injection pump
E	Leak off from main engine injection pump
F	Leak off from GUE fuel injectors
G	Lower tank vents to upper fuel tanks
H	Lower tanks balance pipes
J	GUE supply pressure relief valve fuel return

LEFT The complex pipework involved in moving fuel around the engine.

temperatures; it had been estimated that the maximum temperature would be around 300°C, but it was then discovered that they could reach 650°C. This led to the requirement for the pistons to be oil cooled, which in turn adversely affected the fuel combustion. The fuel injection system was a critical component in allowing the L60 to deliver the 700bhp (later 720 then 750) required. Once oil cooling of the pistons was introduced, combustion heat was reduced, which went against the requirement for burning multi-fuels. Power output was also restricted by poor air flow to the engine, a number of design factors limiting output to 650bhp. It was realised that the inefficiencies of the air filtration and delivery systems, plus the exhaust, were together responsible for losing around 20bhp. The design of the fuel injectors themselves was hampered – yet again – by the multi-fuel requirement, and was much simplified when, finally and belatedly, the decision was made in November 1963 to optimise the engine for diesel only.

Using a CI engine meant that a lot more air was required than with a 4-stroke, and cleaning of the air in dusty conditions was to prove a real challenge. Simply finding enough space within the engine compartment for the air filters and exhaust system was a headache, but getting this right was critical, as L60 performance was

very sensitive to changes with both. Sealing the air cleaner body to the side of the engine block was another difficulty. To achieve efficient filtration, two stages were used: firstly, cyclonic dust extraction 'swirled' the larger particles out of the air flow, where they could be scavenged by an electrical fan. Secondly, the air then passed through a barrier filter element, and again, much trial and error was expended in working out the best material to use, and how often the crews should manually knock out the dust from the element. The original design only allowed for air to be drawn into

BELOW If you want more complexity then look no further than the Fuel Injection Pump (FIP) on the side of the engine.
(TM 10065.078 and 087)

ABOVE The L60 was referred to as a powerpack, as it could be removed and run-up on a test bench, but the TN12 transmission was usually taken off separately.

the engine through the inlet louvres on the rear decks. In part as a result of suggestions made by the Israelis, a 'turret-breathing' system was introduced, which drew air through the turret first, and had the effect of acting as a pre-filter and lessening the amount of dust entering the first stage. Air was drawn into the engine via cable-operated flaps in the engine bulkhead. When operating closed down in NBC conditions, air was drawn through the engine louvres as per the original design.

The original design of the exhaust system had three silencers for each side of the engine, laid over the top of the gearbox and hinged for access. This was not very successful as the gearbox compartment overheated and the silencers developed a high back-pressure. Redesign of the rear of the hull added an external exhaust box containing the silencers, with through pipes from the engine running on top of the gearbox. Later, the gearbox louvres were redesigned to allow an expansion box to be mounted above the gearbox.

The cooling requirements of the engine were initially underestimated; this led to the realisation that larger radiators were needed, along with oil heat exchangers and cooling fans, again adding weight. An interesting anecdote can be told here: the engine designers discovered that the military instructors were teaching their students that a deliberate design feature was that the left-hand radiator always ran cool.

The designers knew that this was not so; investigations showed that although the cooling system was meant to accept 25 gallons of coolant, in fact only a maximum of 18 gallons could go into the system. Further investigations revealed that, for years, the L60 had been operating with a huge airlock, equivalent to 7 gallons of coolant and leading to a massive inefficiency in the system. Bleed valves were fitted and the problem was solved. Another story relates to the tendency of the L60 to shed fan belts, which led to a 'classic case of treating the effect rather than the cause', by introducing stronger belts, and by varying the design from v-belt, through toothed belt, to the final design of multi-vee. Strengthening the belts just transferred the problem to the rear engine gear case, which then began to break, and, as a result, the newly strengthened belts had to be weakened by drilling holes in them. Ultimately, it was found that the real problem was the sprag clutch fitted to each fan hub to allow it to decelerate slowly under control; these were malfunctioning and transferring intermittently high loads to the belts, causing them to break. Once the real problem was identified the clutches were removed, save for the left-hand one which operated only when the GUE was running without the ME.

By July 1964, FVRDE had managed to develop an engine running at an impressive 760bhp, but it was terribly unreliable, and it was clear that solving reliability issues were more important than producing raw power. The Mk 4 engine came out in 1965, but was restricted to 585bhp. In 1966, even as the tank was nearing entry into service and as a result of the continuing difficulties in making the engine both powerful and reliable, FVRDE held a symposium to discuss potential L60 replacements; all leading engine manufacturers were invited and a specification issued. The multi-fuel requirement was thankfully relaxed, but no alternative engine could be found for the tank, so the UK was stuck with the L60.[9] One thing that was helpful at the time was the criticisms made by potential export customers, and the demands (and sometimes suggestions) from them, which concentrated minds and certainly

9   The possibility of turbocharging the L60 had been investigated in 1963, but it was thought to be too complicated to be realistic.

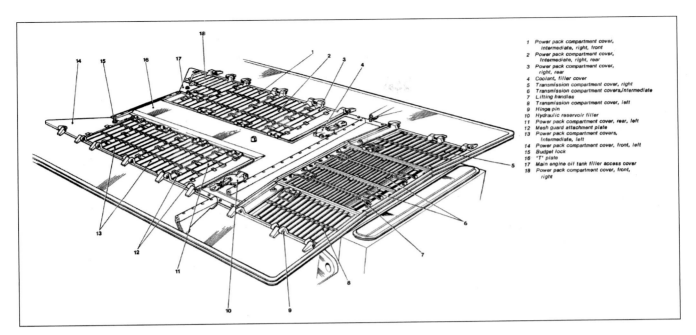

helped to persuade the Treasury to release funds. (When the L60 was first defined in 1958, the military had asked for a conventional diesel engine from an unspecified European country to be developed in parallel in case the L60 proved troublesome, but the Treasury refused to fund it. Oh, the benefits of hindsight. …)

ABOVE The layout of the louvres and engine decks, showing the later version with the raised transmission decks adopted to allow an expansion box to be used.

BELOW The coolant system: the GUE connected into the ME system by self-sealing couplings.

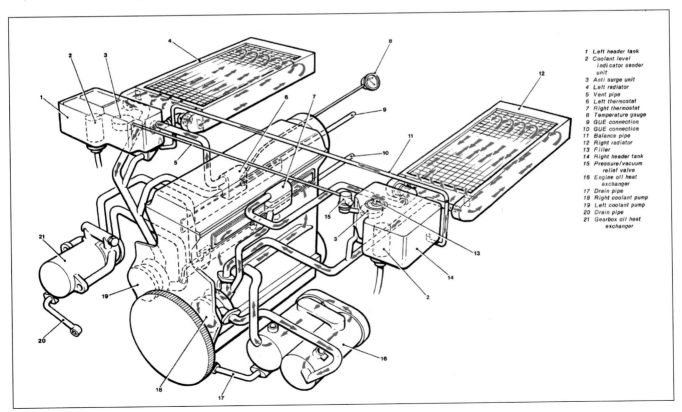

RIGHT AND FAR
RIGHT Two views of
the L60 shown with
one radiator up (for
maintenance) and the
other down (operating
position). (TM
100065.001, 016, 072)

A whole series of programmes were attempted over the years to perfect the L60 and its associated automotive systems; these were technically complicated, involved much trial and error, and took years to work through. Exercise SCOTCH MIST (frustration clearly showing in the choice of name) in 1967 aimed to increase both engine life and reliability, and the FLEETFOOT programme the following year was an attempt to try to reach the desired 750bhp; in the event, 720 was reached, by increasing crankshaft speed from 2,100 to 2,250rpm; redesigning the liner ports to improve air flow; introducing the low-loss air cleaner; and modifying the fuel injection system – again – to suit the other changes.

Exercises DARK MORN and HIGH NOON were carried out from the late 1960s into early 1970 to improve performance and increase durability and reliability. As a result, what was termed as the 'optimum engine' was able to be specified for further development. Also known as the P21, by autumn 1975 it had been run on a test-bed for 400 hours without any form of failure. It was then run on a tank where it completed 1,700 miles before a coolant leak occurred. It was clear to all involved that a soap opera was in progress, and more attempts had been made in 1972 and 1973 to source an alternative engine to the L60, but these were just as unsuccessful as previously, and so the L60 development had to continue.

Exercise SUNDANCE was then conceived as a means of proving that the optimum engine could cope with realistic conditions, using a set standard called the 'battlefield day'. Nine engines to the P21 standard were built, but although they performed faultlessly on test-beds, they failed when used in vehicles in battlefield conditions.[10] It was concluded that the engines were able to flex within the hull, leading to seal failures and coolant leakages that did not occur on the test-beds. It was felt that, if this problem could be solved, the optimum engine was the way forward, as in other respects it was holding up well, and around 2,000 miles MDBF could be expected at this point. Therefore, a new interim standard was specified in August 1977, designated the Mk 9A engine (known as the 10A with a modified blower for export tanks), which incorporated the poly-vee fan belt.

At around this time statistics were compiled from the 148 Chieftains in 2nd Armoured Division taking part in Exercise SPEARPOINT in Germany in 1976. It was estimated that with Chieftain moving on its own tracks (as opposed to static running, which presented less challenges), for every 100 miles covered, 10% would break down and require repairs taking longer than 48 hours. This was not good – a typical unit could thus be expected to be deprived of 20% of its tanks for a significant period after moving 200 miles over a two-day period. The MDBF for the L60 calculated in 1976 was only around 1,000 miles.[11] In order to assist with fault identification

10 In order to quickly identify different engine configurations under trial, the top casings were painted in a coded colour, including red, yellow and orange.

11 One of the planning assumptions used with Chieftain was that each tank would average 800 miles per year, and that the fleet availability rate was to be 80%, rising to 90% with 24 hours' notice; a lack of spare parts meant this was rarely possible.

through statistics, the REME in Germany maintained a data record card logging the history of every L60 in service, no small administrative burden but ultimately helpful.

By October 1977 what seemed to be a breakthrough had taken place: three new engines had been run to 4,000 miles using the battlefield-day criteria without malfunction – one engine eventually clocking up 6,376 battlefield miles before failing. It was then discovered that the existing engine blocks were unable to be modified to the new standard, and thus new blocks had to be specified in February 1978 for the Mk 11A powerpacks. The rebuild programme for these started in 23 base workshops in Wetter, BAOR, in January 1979, using new blocks from Leyland. The need for the highest standards of workshop hygiene in both engine construction and servicing was emphasised, as these areas had been proved to contribute to some of the failures.

On completion of SUNDANCE, a proposal was then made that, because the engines were now using a liner called the 'interference fit' or 'tight liner', piston O rings might be unnecessary; if this could be proved to be so, many of the old engine blocks might be able to be used after all. A trial of four engines without O rings proved the wisdom of this by achieving well over 4,000 miles each, and the Mk 13A (14A for export) was born. With BAOR running on Mk 11A and 13A powerpacks (around 600 had been fitted by April 1981) a noticeable increase in reliability was immediately recorded.

Engineering experts were invited to observe tank drivers in action, and concluded that it

was possible to define the good driver from the, well, not-so-good. (The author was certainly one of the latter.) A good driver would be able to 'balance' the revs when changing gear, and when viewed from the side would maintain the hull in a horizontal posture. The unskilled driver, however, would make the engine either whine (over-revving) or labour (under-revving), which would be visible by the hull nose and rear pitching up and down when changing gear. It was recommended that this evidence be used to retrain drivers as necessary, as good driving was likely to be much less damaging to the pack and transmission. It was also clear to

ABOVE D Sqn 3RTR: Sgt Tony Broom and the REME 'Tiffy' (Artificer SSgt) consider what can be done to get the tank 'back on the road'. The REME tradesmen supporting Chieftain were quite outstanding at keeping the tanks running, and facilitating innovative repairs.

BELOW LEFT AND BELOW Exercise KEY FLIGHT 1989: two shots of the same pack lift, conducted out in the open. Wherever possible, lifts were carried out at night, under cover and with minimum light and noise.
(Courtesy Carl Schulze)

everyone that the tank as a whole performed better when it was being used fairly hard, and did not appreciate long periods of inactivity: the frequent Northern Ireland tours undertaken by armoured regiments in the infantry role from 1969 on were at least partially responsible for such idleness and lower reliability, as well as a reduction of skill levels within crews.

Engine runaways caused by the uncontrolled burning of leaking fuel inside the pack were not uncommon, and the cry of 'Runaway!' announced not only what was happening to the engine, but also indicated the safe action to be taken by personnel in the vicinity. It would lead to everyone in the area putting maximum distance between themselves and the offending engine and then taking cover, before the engine exploded in a shower of metal and a rain of components, followed by frantic firefighting. When an L60 on bench test ran away and blew up in 5 Armoured Workshop in Soest in May 1978, it started a fire which burned down the test-bed facility and severely damaged other parts of the workshop.

The TN12 gearbox

Another source of much trouble and anguish was the gearbox. The TN12 was revolutionary, featuring a semi-automatic gear change system designed to make driving easier. It certainly did that – when it worked. The TN12 was based upon the TN10 design proposed for the cancelled FV300 light tank project, and was designed and manufactured by Self-Changing Gears Ltd. It was of the Merritt–Wilson type; that is, the gear change was based upon a system designed by Major Walter Wilson, and the steering by Herbert Merritt. (Another story that one would constantly hear on the tank park was that 'the man who invented it went mad'.) The basic design was sound for a tank of the specified maximum 45-ton weight and the first example successfully completed its bench tests in September 1959. Unfortunately, the many delays in the L60 programme badly affected the transmission development, as the early engines were breaking down so often that most running was done on the road, and faults within the extremely complicated gearbox caused by the much more demanding cross-country running and heavier tank were not discovered until late in the day. By October 1963, only three gearboxes had successfully completed more than 500 miles, and then on prototypes which had been restricted to 1,800rpm using the low-powered early engines. The prototype vehicles all spent a substantial amount of their lives in various workshops receiving the numerous modifications to bring them up to the 'latest' standard – which, of course, was constantly changing – and therefore even more time was lost.

By late 1962 it had become apparent that gearboxes were suffering from overheating,

RIGHT A typical FTX scene recognisable to all Chieftain crews – the REME working in the gearbox compartment of the author's tank, whilst the local schoolchildren pay a visit.

partly because the exhaust systems shared the transmission compartment, partly due to inadequate mechanical cooling arrangements and lastly because of poor air louvres. These were solved by redesign, but it was becoming clear that part of the problem was more difficult to remedy – the transmission had been designed for a tank of 45 tons, and it was now much heavier than that and still growing.

Other systems

Ironically, after ruining the design of the engine to fulfil the multi-fuel requirement, the fuel gauge fitted to the instrument panel was completely useless, either giving false readings or no reading at all. After some investigations it was decided that it would involve simply too much effort, time and money to introduce a better version, and so nothing was done. Crews simply adopted the maxim of topping up the tanks as often as they could, and dipsticks were provided in each of the four filler caps to allow an accurate measure to be taken if necessary; running out of fuel was a crime, and would lead to the commander involved being seriously disciplined, even sacked.

A new track comprised 96 links, and sprockets were always changed at the same time as the track. The track stretched in use,

ABOVE A 17/21L crew tightening the tracks, a frequent task which was necessary to make steering easier and reduce the likelihood of throwing a track when turning. *(Courtesy Andy Brend)*

GETTING HAMMERED

By Tpr R.J. Taylor 3RTR

When I joined my regiment in 1978 from the Junior Leader's Regiment RAC, my first weeks were spent as a fireman on Green Goddesses in Edinburgh, as the firemen were on strike. As soon as normal work restarted in Tidworth, I was lucky to be put straight on a Chieftain Driving and Maintenance (D&M) Course, which qualified me as a full crewman – with a decent pay rise – at the tender age of 17½. Even luckier, my tank commander was a great guy called Cpl Alf Moore, who was a real wizard in all things D&M and who helped me massively; in truth, he often did the repairs and maintenance that I should really have done myself. One day as I walked past him in the tank park, I saw him lying half under the tank in a very strange position, clearly tinkering as usual – or so I thought. About ten minutes later I passed him again, and he failed to answer my greeting. This was unusual as he was a really nice chap, and then I realised that he had not changed position since I first saw him. He was unconscious. Dragging him out, he had a huge bruise right in the centre of his forehead, with a lump the size of a duck's egg. When he came to he was able to explain what had happened. He had been using a hammer to knock out the large bolts holding the suspension bump stops in position, and had missed the bolt head and hit the rubber pad instead, causing the hammer to rebound and knock him out!

RIGHT AND FAR RIGHT Track bashing. Hard, honest labour if ever there was, not something that anyone exactly enjoyed doing, but there was a certain satisfaction when the job was over. Sprockets were always changed when a new track was fitted. A good crew could complete a full track and sprocket change under tactical conditions overnight – the author knows because he's done it.

ABOVE Using the sprocket to winch the new track over the idler and top rollers.
(TM 5931D6)

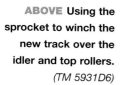

requiring adjustment of the idler (aka track-adjusting) wheel to take up the slack. When there was no more adjustment in the wheel a link had to be removed. When the track was down to 92 links, over-pitched sprockets with a different profile were fitted, and the track was finally condemned at 88–90 links. Two spare links could be carried on hooks fitted to the exhaust box on the rear of the hull, although these were not part of the tool kit; a few spare track pins and retaining circlips were always carried. The track links themselves were cast at K&L Steelfounders (KL) of Letchworth; in the early 1980s, problems were encountered with track links, a few of which were breaking up unexpectedly, leading to the whole fleet being grounded on safety reasons. This led to an investigation to determine the cause, which was done and which surprised everyone involved. It seems that the links were cast in one part of KL's factory, and were then taken on the back of an open trailer to a different location

LEFT Tpr Andy Hayden applies a sledgehammer to a seized top roller; note the use of the jacks (from two different tanks as each tank only carried one) to prevent having to split the track. Cpl – later RSM – Andy Fisher supervises.
(Courtesy Andy Fisher)

ABOVE The hull of P1 was used for firing trials at Kirkcudbright in January 1967. Eleven HESH were fired at her and the poor old girl was badly knocked about, but this is the clearest surviving period photograph so far discovered which shows the original suspension unit design based on Centurion, with the separate top rollers.

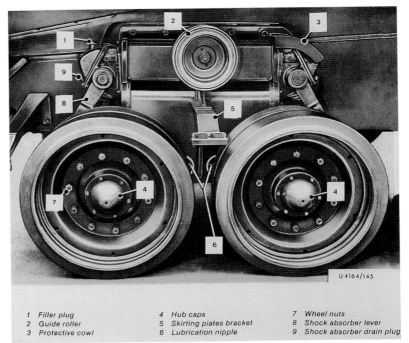

U 4164/145

1	Filler plug	4	Hub caps	7	Wheel nuts
2	Guide roller	5	Skirting plates bracket	8	Shock absorber lever
3	Protective cowl	6	Lubrication nipple	9	Shock absorber drain plug

ABOVE The Horstmann suspension unit. Whereas British Army tanks only had shock absorbers/dampers fitted to the first unit on either side, the 5/3 (P) export tanks had them on the first and third pairs.

BELOW A more severe test, but easily negotiated. When crossing knife-edge and vertical-step-type obstacles, putting the gun over the side prevented the gun bouncing off the elevation and depression limits as the hull pitched up and down. *(Courtesy Andy Brend)*

to be heat-treated to give them the necessary strength. On the way, a few links would often fall off the trailer, and the driver just left them there. When he next passed, this time carrying a load of links that had been through the heat-treatment process, he picked up the untreated links and added them to his load, thereby mixing up a few understrength links with the majority, which were of the correct quality.

Using Horstmann suspension units based upon those fitted to Centurion were the first choice for the prototypes of Chieftain, as the design possessed a number of advantages over other systems, and in particular torsion bars.[12] Torsion bar systems add height and take up much-needed volume inside the hull; additionally, changing them can be a major challenge. As the Horstmann units were externally mounted, they did not use up volume inside the hull, and were also more resistant to mine attack. When damaged, they could be replaced fairly easily and quickly in the field; maintenance was also simple.

Strengthened suspensions then quickly became necessary as the tank's weight increased. Some of the prototypes were modified, with a new design of Horstmann unit being used. These featured shock absorbers/ dampers on the front stations, and the top

---

12 Hydrogas or Hydrostrut was too immature at this time to be a serious contender.

ABOVE The approved method of lifting the heavy roadwheels on or off – getting the inner one off took even more strength and technique.

BELOW Much the same job – but made so much more unpleasant by the conditions. The sprocket rings have been removed, possibly to fit the over-pitched type.

rollers were incorporated into the top of each unit. The final drive was both redesigned at the same time and raised. The idlers were also redesigned, the earliest version having looked very similar to the Centurion type. Larger roadwheels based on Centurion were also fitted. This proved successful, and the new design was used with no major modifications for the rest of the tank's service life.

THE POWER OF LITERATURE

Maj David Viccars 3RTR

Whilst on exercise on the SLTA in Germany in the mid-1980s, my Chieftain tank, having performed wonderfully for days, suddenly ground to a halt with all the electrics down … disastrously, even the Boiling Vessel (BV) wasn't working. It was quickly identified that there was most likely a problem with the hull main junction box, the box through which electrical power was distributed around the tank. Sure enough, as the turret slowly turned to expose this box situated on the hull wall, most of the 18 circuit breakers (CBs) had popped out. Easy, we thought, push them back in and off we go … but nope, out they popped again. After a radio chat with our 'Bluebell', the REME section, we were told to find the user handbook. This was a very grubby and stained 3in-thick A4 book. The answer though was not to be found within its covers: nevertheless, the REME had devised a clever solution. When applied to the junction box, it neatly fitted over all the CBs at the same time thus holding them in place … so with the turret at the required angle and the loader pressing the book firmly against the CBs, we had full electrical power and were able to motor the five miles back to our leaguer (with the BV now fully functioning) for a full repair where the offending component – which was short circuiting – was replaced. That was one of the great joys of Chieftain; quite often there were 'get you home' actions which the crew or REME could take to keep the tank operative.

ABOVE The hull rear. From the left, the Mk 1 configuration, followed by two variants of the later layout, typical of Mk 3 onwards, and of earlier marks of tank that had been reworked. *(Courtesy Keith Paget)*

BELOW The refuse ejector fitted to the left-hand hull wall, designed to allow the crew to get rid of rubbish when closed down under NBC conditions.

ABOVE Both transmission decks are open, with the steering brake reservoir and GUE exhaust visible in the corner. One radiator has been raised exposing the top of the air cleaner. Note the amount of debris, especially leaves, which gather in the radiator matrix and have to be regularly cleaned out.

BELOW Inside the hull (fighting compartment) with the turret and basket removed. The seven hull charge bins and the ready charge bin (vertical with three lids) for 42 charges can be seen, and the projectile racks have been stowed with HESH. The seat visible is the gunner's, and the rear of the driver's seat can just be seen in the image on the right.

Chapter Three

Turret, lethality and survivability

────●────

Chieftain was, above all its other virtues, renowned for the accuracy and penetration achieved by the remarkable 120mm gun. This used a revolutionary – for tanks – system of bag-charges, which made ammunition handling in the confined space of the turret much easier, as well as improving survivability in the event of a penetration. The tank was also extremely well protected by its armour, which was improved as the tank was developed.

OPPOSITE Looking down the business end of the 120mm gun – not a prospect to be relished by an enemy. Chieftain's gun required little in the way of modifications whilst it was in service, but the fire control systems and associated equipment were subject to a whole series of improvements, as was the ammunition.

55

Armour protection

Chieftain's design characteristics called for it to mount the 'best available armour within the overall weight limit'. This necessarily constrained the amount of armour that could be used, and, as we have discovered, the amount of armour fitted to both the turret front and glacis had to be reduced in order to remove weight. Despite this, it remained an extremely well-protected tank, with greater all-round survivability than the heavy tanks of its time. The turret consisted of a large well-shaped casting which provided protection for the front half of the turret, with flat plates of Rolled Homogenous Armour (RHA) welded to it to form the sides and rear bustle. The frontal armour was 280mm thick, which had been proved to be easily capable of defeating the 100mm APHE round used by the Soviets on their T54/55 series of medium tanks.

BELOW The two turrets tested in 1959: the turret without a mantlet (bottom) proved to be the superior design. The turrets of the FV4202 Experimental Vehicle and 105mm FV4201 were manufactured by FH Lloyd and Co. Ltd and were delivered at a unit price of £1,625 each.

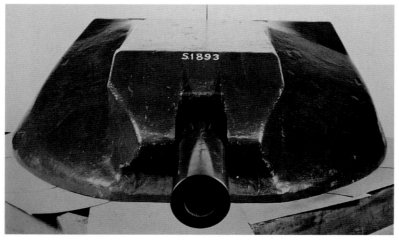

Alternative gun mountings and turret fronts, with and without conventional mantlets, were tested in firing trials in April 1959; both were made by FH Lloyd (FHL) of Wednesbury, who later produced the armoured turret and glacis castings for the FV4202 turret and then the service tank, hence the FHL markings found on those components. (Two other companies also made armour castings for Chieftain: English Steel Castings (ESC) and KL, who also cast the tracks.) The experimental turrets were tested by firing Russian 100mm APHE from an SU-100 (borrowed from the Bovington Tank Museum) at only 100 yards range, as well as with British 20-pounder ammunition. The design without a mantlet resisted all attacks, whereas the turret with a mantlet was holed and the gun mounting jammed. The mantletless design was selected, and the maximum frontal armour thickness of 280mm specified, which, because of its shape and slope, gave an effective equivalent thickness of 500mm.

Over 20 years later, in 1981, British personnel from the International Military Services (IMS) organisation, including an expert from MVEE, were invited by Saddam Hussein's Iraqi government to examine the 190 or so Chieftains that they had captured from the Iranians, who, since the fall of the Shah, were considered to be in the unfriendly camp. It was found that about 70% of the knocked-out tanks (the exact number examined was not stated) had been hit predominantly by 115mm Fin-Stabilised Armour-Piercing Discarding Sabots (FSAPDS) from T62s, plus some 100mm from T55s, as well as guided missile and RPG7 strikes. It was thought that most of the tanks had been abandoned before being hit and then hit at quite close ranges, and that the standard of serviceability and tactics employed by the Iranian crews had not allowed the tanks to make use of their capabilities. Nonetheless, a worrying picture emerged: of 88 strikes from 115mm, 71 had penetrated the armour, often on the sides but some had got through the thickest protection at the front. Of seven recorded RPG7 hits, none had penetrated. It was estimated by the assessors that about 80 of the Chieftains could be brought back into service after some minor repairs, 30 needed workshop attention, with a similar number requiring a base overhaul, and the remainder were beyond economic repair. Although the tanks were often badly damaged, the team were pleased to note that, in all cases, the gunner's telescopes had remained serviceable, meaning that the tanks could still shoot with reasonable accuracy.

But what really focused the attention of the British staff officers was the fact that Chieftain, proof against T55, was very vulnerable to the newer T62, and worse still, would need increased frontal protection to defeat the latest Soviet tank gun, the 125mm. The British assessment of the penetrative performance of the two Soviet guns when fired point-blank at 'normal' (perpendicular) against RHA was as follows:

	Steel core FSAPDS	Tungsten core FSAPDS
115mm (T62)	272mm	360mm
125mm (T72)	420mm	475mm

Although this represented the absolute worst case – point-blank – it presented worrying evidence that one of Chieftain's two greatest attributes had fallen behind in the gun v armour race. This meant that a consistent thickness of 500mm of armour was necessary to defeat all these natures; Chieftain already had that amount in certain areas on the turret front, but the thickness varied and the minimum there was 240mm; on the hull the 18° sloped armour glacis casting gave an equivalent maximum thickness of 388mm. What was required to defeat the worst-case threat ammunition was a consistent minimum of 500mm over the entire turret front.

As a result, in December 1981 a project was initiated to up-armour the turret front of Chieftain. This was known originally as CAA – Chieftain Additional Armour – and was approved as Operational Emergency (OE) GSR 3988 in May 1984. It was better known as Stillbrew, the name taken from the military lead, Colonel Still and from an MVEE engineer, John Brewer, much in the manner of the naming convention for the Sten gun of the Second World War. The area that needed the protection was the front half of the turret, or, in other words, from nine o'clock through to three o'clock. The protection could not go down to the bottom of the turret due to the

ABOVE One of the Iranian Chieftains in 1981 showing multiple hits on the turret. (TM 6077C6)

need to traverse through 360°, and the height of the engine decks made full depth protection impossible. This could be partially overcome by fitting additional armoured collars to the hull front, either side of the driver's periscope, but the area under the panels remained vulnerable to a chance hit.

During 1983, MVEE trials had shown that the desired performance could be obtained, and better still, that resistance to Chemical Energy (CE) ammunition (tank-fired High Explosive Anti-Tank (HEAT)) was also enhanced. Following formal project approval, during 1985 prototype armour packs mounted on to three turrets were subjected to firing trials at Kirkcudbright using British 105mm APFSDS and 120mm APFSDS; the former was resisted point-blank and the latter (which was a better penetrator than the Soviet 125mm) at around 1,000m. In June 1985 the drawings were finalised, and the following month financial authority was given for 250 kits to be produced by ROFL.[13] In order to fit the turret panels, the turret central lifting eye (used during gun pull-back) and the smoke dischargers had to be relocated, with the left-hand discharger given a hinged bracket in order to allow access to the engine decks when traversed over the rear. The existing four front-engine louvre doors had to be replaced with six smaller doors, four hinged and two sliding. Two tanks (00EB67 and 01EB65) were used for 'trundle' and 'firing from' trials, to confirm the effects upon fire control, mobility, habitability

---

13 In 1986, while the project was ongoing, ROFL was bought by Vickers.

SECRET

ABOVE An early mock-up of Stillbrew, using a model of a prototype Chieftain, to show how additional armour might be fitted to the front of the Chieftain, to defeat the latest Soviet tank ammunition. It was a complicated task, as the panels had to fit the complex turret curvature without impeding the use of sights and other components.

to the turret face – a composite construction but certainly not Chobham armour as is sometimes stated. In fact, the use of Chobham was discussed and would clearly have been the best technical solution, but would have necessitated either a new turret or at the least very considerable modifications, and so was ruled out on both cost and time reasons. Due to design constraints and the varying turret profiles which came from three different casting foundries, the consistent 500mm thickness overall could not be achieved, with it varying from 480mm to 540mm; however, the final design was considered sufficient to stand a good chance of resisting the successor Soviet 125mm round (tungsten monobloc and sheathed staballoy, which was postulated as being able to penetrate around 530mm point-blank), and each panel individually was considered able to take at least two hits. Ballistic 'fences' were built into the design to help prevent spall caused by an impact from being deflected into the vulnerable sights. The armour packs came in five pieces for the turret and two for the hull, and added 2.25 tons to the tank. Although mobility was impaired to some degree and servicing was estimated to take 17% longer, these were considered to be prices worth paying.

and so on. By January 1986, both tanks had successfully completed 6,000km trials – an unintended tribute to the increased reliability of the L60 by this time.

The armour packs were made of RARDE 823 steel and mounted on to concealed studs, with laminated rubber seals on the insides mating

The conversion kits were made in Leeds

RIGHT A completed Stillbrew turret showing the trough necessary to allow the gunner's emergency telescope (SU) to be used, including the protective rubber bung on the chain used to shield the object lens when not in use. The area of the lower turret not able to be protected by additional armour is very apparent.

and the majority were sent to BAOR where 23 base workshops at Wetter fitted them to tanks as they were rotated there for overhaul, with the No 11 NBC pack being retrofitted to most tanks at the same time to turn them into the Mk 10. The first Mk 10 to enter service was issued in mid-1986 to the Commanding Officer (CO) of 3RTR, Lt Col Mike Napper, who probably pulled strings as he had previously been the deputy PM Chieftain; unfortunately this was announced in two forces newspapers in BAOR, which caused embarrassment as the project was still classified as secret. In the same period, even as Chieftain was starting to be phased out of service in favour of Challenger, Stillbrew Chieftain with TOGS – the Mk 11 – was to become the final front-line variant.

The 120mm gun

Once liquid propellant had been found to be unfeasible after the 1953 trials, a bag-charge system was always the front runner, with a 105mm gun using bag-charges originally specified in 1954. As space inside the turret was very limited, with a low roof and a large breech to contend with, as well as water-jacketed ammunition containers, a way had to be found to limit the length of ammunition components; it was decided that 27in was the maximum that could be handled. This ruled out using conventional fixed ammunition, so only two solutions were possible: semi-fixed or separate. As the former offered no advantages over the latter, and indeed would probably slow down the speed of loading, separate bag-charge ammunition was chosen. This required the design not only of a new family of ammunition but also the means of igniting the bag-charge and of sealing the breech, hence the development of the Vent Tube (VT) and the obturators.[14] It was later claimed that loader fatigue was reduced, as each piece of separate ammunition weighed considerably less than the equivalent 105mm round, important for maintaining high rates of fire over long periods – vital in war but something not really tested in the NATO gunnery competitions …

When examining the design of the gun for FV4201, one of the most important considerations was choosing the optimum calibre. It had to be capable of defeating the (then) current Soviet medium tank at 2,000yd, and the Soviet heavy tank at 'as long a range as possible'. It also had to show potential for improvement, principally through improved ammunition. Twelve guns between 105mm and

ABOVE The two collars fitted to the hull, which reduced but did not remove the vulnerable area below the turret armour.
(Courtesy Robert Lockie)

BELOW Firing now! A late model (Mk 11) Chieftain on the ranges at Castlemartin in Wales. The 120mm gun was designed to kill Soviet armour at long range, not to win NATO competitions.

---

14 An attempt was made to achieve obturation using a 6in deep brass stub case – as later used on the Rheinmetall 120mm – but it could not be made reliable or safe, so ring obturation was pursued instead.

130mm were examined before 120mm was recommended for development in December 1955. (The actual calibre was an imperial 4.7in, which was 119.38mm when expressed metrically, and so was rounded up for simplicity.) This became the experimental 120mm X23E2/3 gun which was over 300kg lighter than its two nearest rivals and, as we know, weight was all-important. But performance counted too, and it was estimated that the 120mm would be able to defeat 120mm of RHA at 60° at 2,000yd, or 150mm using HESH at any combat range. This was proved to be the case when it entered service; by comparison, the 105mm Centurion L7 gun (also used on Leopard, M60 and early M1) could only defeat the standard NATO medium tank target (T54/55) at 1,250yd, and could not reliably defeat the NATO heavy tank target (T10) at any range.

In service form the X23 became the 'Ordnance Breech Loading [BL] 120mm Tank L11A1', later developed into the A2, A3 and A5 versions. The service guns, starting with the L11A1, fitted to the prototypes and Mk 1s only, featured a nickel-chrome-molybdenum steel monobloc barrel, and were made at ROF Nottingham. The gun design offers us a fascinating glimpse into the intricacies of tank design: as it had been found that most loaders were right-handed and so preferred loading using the right arm, this meant that the loader would be best positioned in the left of the turret, so the gunner and commander would need to be on the other side. This in turn meant the sights would be offset to the right

BELOW This is the 120mm gun barrel – honestly! It is shown in early ingot stage, before being drawn out and extensively machined to form the finished barrel.

of the line of the barrel, so therefore the gun rifling had to have a clockwise twist in order to compensate. Every decision made in one area had implications in others. As another example, the mantletless design meant that the barrel would need to be changed through the rear of the turret, which affected the design of that area and the NBC pack.

Three types of ramming system for the projectile were tried. The initial idea was impractical, and involved an electro-mechanical rammer which was meant to push the projectile fully forward. Unfortunately, it was unreliable as well as adding 90kg to an already overweight tank. The trial crews disliked it and resorted to charge-ramming, using the bagcharge to push the projectile fully home. The Ordnance Board experts – mainly with an RA background – were opposed to this, thinking it was unsafe, and tried to have it banned, although the more realistic RAC experts pointed out that crews in battle would resort to this anyway if the rammer failed them. Later trials and a slight redesign of the bagcharges proved that it was both safe and speeded up the loading time, and so it was adopted. (The third method was an interim solution, only used whilst the safety of charge-ramming was being tested: this was a hand rammer, consisting of a wooden pole 46in long, hinged in the middle with a sliding brass sleeve to make it rigid, and a brass plate on the end that contacted the base of the projectile. The crews hated it.)

The initial gunnery performance report was published in July 1962; broadly the tank had impressed, as it was both accurate and hard-hitting, although serious concerns were expressed about the efficiency – or otherwise – of the No 11 cupola. Additionally, all three MGs had performed poorly. Also in 1962, during a user gunnery demonstration fired against targets at known ranges out to 2,000m,[15] the crews managed to achieve 17 out of 21 first-round hits using APDS (81%), and a creditable 20 out of 22 first- or second-round hits using HESH, thus proving what an inherently accurate gun had been selected. In 1967 a more demanding test was conducted to establish the chances of a first-round hit at longer ranges

15 Chieftain was the first British vehicle to use metres rather than yards as the basic measurement of range.

% CHANCES OF A FIRST-ROUND HIT USING APDS

TARGET	RANGE (M)		
	2,000	2,500	3,000
2.3m × 2.3m (representing a full-size tank)	48	32	22
0.9m × 1.5m (representing a tank turret)	16	11	6

(beyond 2,000m), using APDS against full size and tank turret targets in combat conditions where the initial range was not known – see the table above.

The figures obtained showed an understandable reduction in hit probability; not knowing the range to the target was the key factor which led to a miss, and the fire control equipment (No 38 × 8 gunner's sight and .50 RG) were working beyond their design specifications. Partly as a result of trials like these, but mainly because of the need to improve the chances of hitting long-range and moving targets, the TLS and then the IFCS were developed.

Similarly, the lightweight .30in M73 MGs specified for the coax and commander's use were found to be unreliable. This weapon was also made by General Electric (GE) in the USA and it was intended to be the coax MG on the M48 tank; in US service it was unpopular and prone to jamming. Similar problems were found when it was put on to Chieftain and it became obvious that a more reliable and robust weapon was required. The Belgian-designed FN General-Purpose Machine Gun (GPMG) firing the NATO standard 7.62 × 51mm ammunition was then selected, and developed by the British into the L8 variant for both roles on the tank. However, it was subsequently found that the L8 could not be easily dismounted and used in the infantry role, so in 1968 another version was made, called the L37A1, which had a pistol grip as standard and could be quickly dismounted with the addition of a butt in place of the smaller recoil buffer. The standard infantry L1A2 barrel with foresight and bipod could also be left on the gun when in the cupola mounting, which was modified to allow the new gun to fit. Unlike the other GPMGs in British service, both weapons had a Feed Pawl Depressor fitted to the feed mechanism; this was originally designed in order to allow the loader to feed a belt into the gun without opening the top cover, but it was never used in that manner and only came into use when carrying out the stoppage drill.

120mm ammunition

Firstly, a little background. MA ammunition can be divided into two broad categories. Those projectiles which rely on a combination of their composition, mass and momentum to have the desired effect are known as Kinetic Energy (KE), whereas those which use an explosive or incendiary effect are known as CE. The ammunition used in the 120mm gun is three-piece, meaning that the projectile and propellant is separate, and brass cartridge cases are not required. The first part is the projectile, and the second part is the propellant, which comes in the form of 'bag-charges', either a rigid Nitro-Cellulose/Kraft full cylinder type for KE, or a half-cylinder in an unbleached calico bag for CE. The former is much more water-repellent than the latter, although not completely waterproof, so the charges must always be kept dry to avoid hangfires or misfires.[16] In all cases, the handle used to extract the charge from the stowage (the charge bin) goes into the chamber first after the projectile. The base of each bag-charge contains an igniter pad of a more sensitive propellant, which is ignited by the third component, the electrically fired VT. (In that strange reversed army terminology it is officially called the 'Tube Vent Electric L1A4'(TV). The VT looks rather like a large cartridge case with no bullet fitted and has a nominal calibre of .625in. The three components that make up one complete piece of ammunition – projectile, bag-charge and VT – are referred to as a 'round', the terminology coming from the days of cannonballs.

The KE ammunition family has three main types (aka natures) within it. In very basic

---

16 A hangfire is when there is a delay in firing; a misfire is when the gun does not fire at all.

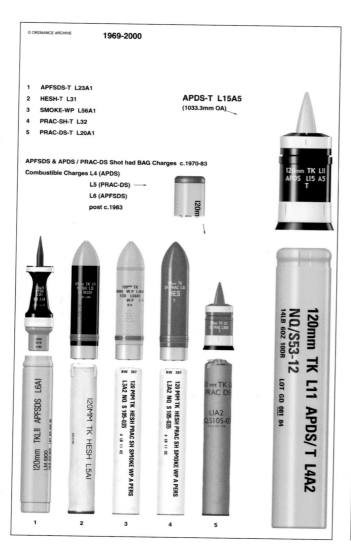

1969-2000

1 APFSDS-T L23A1
2 HESH-T L31
3 SMOKE-WP L56A1
4 PRAC-SH-T L32
5 PRAC-DS-T L20A1

APDS-T L15A5
(1033.3mm OA)

APFSDS & APDS / PRAC-DS Shot had BAG Charges c.1970-83
Combustible Charges L4 (APDS)

L5 (PRAC-DS)
L6 (APFSDS)
post c.1983

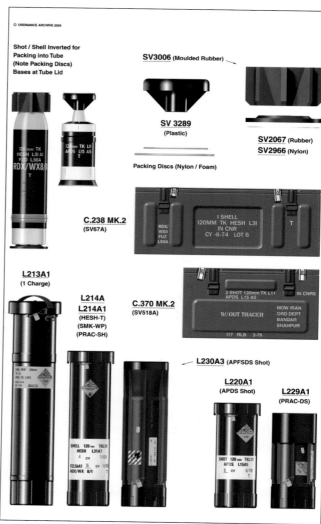

Shot / Shell Inverted for
Packing into Tube
(Note Packing Discs)
Bases at Tube Lid

SV3006 (Moulded Rubber)

SV 3289
(Plastic)

SV2067 (Rubber)
SV2966 (Nylon)

Packing Discs (Nylon / Foam)

C.238 MK.2
(SV67A)

L213A1
(1 Charge)

L214A
L214A1
(HESH-T)
(SMK-WP)
(PRAC-SH)

C.370 MK.2
(SV518A)

L230A3 (APFSDS Shot)

L220A1
(APDS Shot)

L229A1
(PRAC-DS)

ABOVE 120mm L11 TK
ammunition (120mm
L11 BL gun).

ABOVE RIGHT
120mm L11 gun
ammunition packing
(representative
selection only, not to
scale).

terms KE requires a dense penetrator to move at extremely high speed in order to defeat an armoured target. Better performance is generally achieved by increasing the mass and/ or density of the projectile, and/or increasing the speed. The original main armour-defeating nature provided was APDS. This is generally simply called 'sabot', pronounce 'sa-bow' – the word comes from the Flemish for shoe, and refers to the way that high velocity is achieved. A small-calibre central tungsten-carbide sub-projectile (the core) is made up to full 120mm calibre by lightweight discarding pots and/ or petals (the shoes); these fly off after the projectile has left the barrel, leaving the core to hit the target. As it is an armour-defeating nature, the projectile is painted the standard NATO colour of Black. A training version of the round with a lighter steel core is available, as

this has a much smaller safety template that that for APDS, and is also less expensive to manufacture. This is Discarding Sabot/Tracer, known as DS/T. As it is a practice nature, it is painted Deep Saxe Blue (colour code No 216 in the BSC 381c system), as is the top of its corresponding Nitro-Cellulose Kraft (NC/K) bag-charge, which is all that will be seen when it is placed in a charge bin. The white bands around both projectile types are nylon centring bands and their colour is not significant. The APDS weighs 10.5kg and has a muzzle velocity (MV) of 1,370m/s, DS/T is lighter at 5.9kg and, despite using less propellant, is slightly quicker at 1,460m/s.

In the late 1970s it was realised that the APDS projectile would be unable to reliably penetrate the latest Soviet armour, so in June 1978, GSR (OE) 3758 set out the requirements for a new KE nature able to do so. At that time, the scientists at RARDE were developing a new KE projectile known as APFSDS – Armour-Piercing Fin-Stabilised Discarding Sabot, known as 'Fin' for short. This was ready for intensive trials from 1982 to 1984, and was recommended for acceptance in March 1984. In order to fire a fin-stabilised round through a rifled barrel, slipping driving bands were fitted to allow the projectile to rotate at the lower spin rate required. The resulting L23 APFSDS round weighed 8kg and the centre core was a tungsten-nickel alloy dart known as the long rod penetrator. Made at ROF Birtley, it entered service in the mid-1980s, requiring a new set of projectile racks to stow the nature in; the charge bins were unaffected. The fire control system had to be upgraded to account for the ballistic characteristics of the new ammunition; the MV was 1,540m/s, and the TVE L3A1 superseded the L1A4. The L23 extended the life of the L11 gun, as it was able to outperform the Soviet 125mm: remembering that the 125mm with tungsten core was able to penetrate 475mm of RHA point-blank, the L23 could penetrate 450mm at a range of 1,000m. (The Depleted Uranium successor, the L26, used by Challenger 1 in the 1991 war, could penetrate 570mm at the same range.)

All of these KE natures require a (different) full-cylinder bag-charge, each around 27in long. Early versions of the DS/T charge were a blue-coloured cloth bag, but by the early 1980s had been replaced by rigid water-resistant NC/K charges. The top of the APFSDS charge has a hollow cup with the cloth tape handle inside, the cup fits over the orange fin case during loading.

There are also three main CE natures: these are HESH, Squash Head Practice (SH/P) and Smoke. Each has the same ballistic characteristics, with an MV of 670m/s, and all use the same 24in-long half-cylinder cloth-covered bag-charge. HESH stands for High-Explosive Squash Head, and is a dual-purpose nature: it can be used against lightly armoured

RIGHT Firing now! A Mk 2 dozer tank on the ranges in winter. The two men on the turret top are gunnery instructors supervising the crew.
(Courtesy Andrew Chapman)

ABOVE Not brought into British service, the range of ammunition developed for Iranian requirements: a very pointed nose on a **HESH** projectile (third from left), a fin-stabilised **HEAT** projectile (centre) and a nose-fused **Smoke** shell (second from right). On the extreme right is the 120mm Canister nature. This was an anti-personnel nature containing 703 steel pellets and designed for use against massed infantry attacks.

ABOVE 'Ammo bashing', the process of unboxing 120mm ammunition was time-consuming and long-winded. Here, B Sqn 3RTR crews carry it out at Hohne ranges around 1985 under the watchful eye of SSM Stan Wood. The young officer mucking-in in the middle is 2Lt, now Maj Gen, John Patterson.
(Courtesy Andrew Chapman)

vehicles (AVs) such as basic (not up-armoured) T55/T62 series or armoured personnel carriers, and also as an HE nature for engaging troops and soft-skin vehicles, or dug-in anti-tank weapons. It is also extremely effective for knocking holes in reinforced concrete walls. HESH is mainly painted Black, denoting its anti-armour capability, with a Golden Yellow (code 356) nose to show that it has an HE filling. The practice equivalent is SH/P, and is always referred to as 'Shush Pee'. Using the same body as HESH, it has a completely inert non-explosive filling and so is painted overall Deep Saxe Blue. The final CE nature is the Eau-de-Nil (code 216) Smoke shell, again using exactly the same body but filled with a White Phosphorous (WP) composition. A thin Golden Yellow band around the nose denotes the small HE filling

used to burst the shell open on impact. Both HESH and SH/P have tracers fitted in the base to allow the fall of shot to be seen, but Smoke does not, as where it lands will be marked by the emission of copious quantities of dense white smoke. All of the CE shells weigh the same at 17.1kg.

The breech, cradle and recoil system

The MA is officially called the 'Ordnance, Breech Loading, 120mm Tank, L11A1–A7'. The 120mm gun barrel is made of Electro-Slag Refined (ESR) steel, auto-frettaged to deliberately overstress the barrel lining, rifled and then machined to size in a giant lathe. Weighing 1,073kg, the purpose of the barrel is to spin the projectile in order to impart accuracy; behind the rifled portion of the barrel is a plain enlarged cylinder, the chamber, into which the projectile and bag-charge are placed prior to firing. From the A3 onwards, at the muzzle end at 12 o'clock is a flat platform for mounting the MRS mirror and shroud – see below. About one-third down the barrel from the muzzle are two seatings, with eight angled gas ports between them for the fume extractor. Externally at the chamber end are a series of interrupted screw threads, to which the breech ring is attached. When the barrel is worn and needs changing (which it will do after a relatively low number of service KE rounds), the REME will dismantle the breech and remove the old barrel through the rear of the turret, bringing the new barrel in the same way – a long and laborious process.

The main purposes of the breech are to allow safe and rapid loading, and to seal the rear end of the chamber for firing. To do this the breech has two major components, the breech ring and, sliding within the ring, the breech block. The former is of the closed jaw type, the top edge of the jaw forming a curved surface which is the first part of the loading platform. The breech block is of the vertically sliding variety; when open (in the 'load' position), the top curved surface forms the second part of the loading platform with the empty chamber immediately in front of it. When the breech is closed, a matched pair of extremely finely

BELOW The main components of the barrel and breech mechanism; in the upper image the breech is closed, in the lower it is open in the 'load' position.

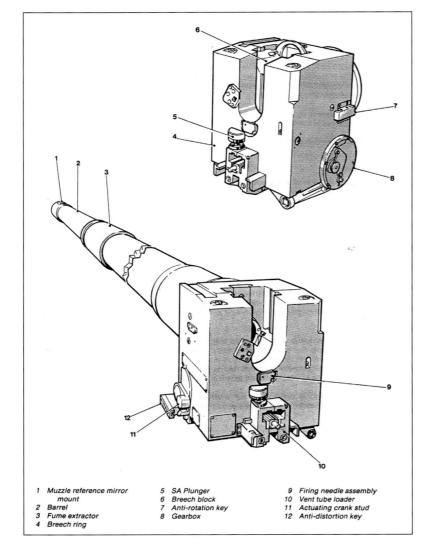

1	Muzzle reference mirror mount	5	SA Plunger	9	Firing needle assembly
2	Barrel	6	Breech block	10	Vent tube loader
3	Fume extractor	7	Anti-rotation key	11	Actuating crank stud
4	Breech ring	8	Gearbox	12	Anti-distortion key

machined steel rings known as obturators, one in the rear of the chamber and one in the face of the breech block, come together under the immense gas pressure on firing to prevent the huge quantities of super-heated gas from escaping rearwards. A number of fail-safe devices are fitted, including an arm which drops down to indicate that the obturator primary seal has failed, and another which indicates that the obturator within the breech block is not fitted; both prevent the loader from pushing a projectile into the chamber.

Immediately under the loading platform on the rear of the breech ring is the Firing Needle Assembly or FNA; this holds one VT ready to be fired and forms part of the firing train – see below. Beneath the FNA at the bottom is a mechanism called the Vent Tube Loader (VTL). The VTL holds a magazine of up to 14 VTs, allowing the loader to feed one VT at the correct point in the loading sequence. Inside and underneath the breech is the mechanism to allow the breech block to open, close and be removed/replaced for cleaning. On the right side is the anti-rotation bracket, which prevents the tendency of the gun to twist counter-clockwise on firing, due to an equal and opposite reaction to the projectile speeding clockwise down the rifling. On the right-hand side (RHS) is a moulded fibreglass safety shield, which prevents the gunner or commander from moving too far to their left and into the 'swept area' of the gun. A circular hole in the shield allows the gunner to access the breech gearbox plunger when assisting in stripping the breech, and a rectangular cut-out allows the commander to operate the emergency MA firing circuit when necessary – in peacetime this can only be used for static firing, because of the real danger of a trapped hand when the gun is stabilised.

The gun cradle has a number of functions. By means of trunnions mounted either side at the front, the cradle can move up to +356mils (20°) in elevation, and −178mils/10° in depression as required (although depression is limited over the sides and especially the rear). The narrowness of the trunnions can be cited as something of a design flaw, as it made achieving a really accurate weapon system quite difficult, certainly more so than with a conventional external mantlet with widely

spaced trunnions. Stabilising such a long barrel when shooting on the move is also difficult. These are two of the reasons (there are more) why the L11 could be outperformed by the Rheinmetall 120mm, or indeed the 105mm L7, in gunnery competitions.

Inside the cradle is the barrel chase, a greased tube that allows the barrel to move rearwards (recoil) and forwards (run-out) on firing. The rear of the barrel of the L11 gun fits within the chase, and as the breech ring is screwed on to the threads at the extreme rear of the barrel, the movement of the gun within the chase is connected to and limited by the recoil system as described below. As can be imagined, when the gun fires there is an enormous amount of force exerted on the trunnions, and this is known as 'trunnion pull'.

Mounted on the cradle is the recoil system for the MA. This comprises two oil-filled hydraulic buffers to absorb much of the recoil energy and limit the length of recoil to only 14in; one is mounted on the top of the cradle in the one o'clock position, the other diagonally opposite underneath. They also provide a feature which slows down the final 1.5in of run-out to prevent metal crashing into metal. In the six o'clock position underneath the cradle is the twin cylinder hydro-pneumatic recuperator; this absorbs the remainder of the recoil energy, and the air pressure within (500psi) keeps the gun in the run-out (ie fully forward) position

ABOVE The loader's view of the breech, with the steel breech block in the up (closed) position within the green breech ring; this gun is mounted on an instructional stand, not in a tank. Visible here are, on the right side: the gun shield, recoil indicator and emergency firing box; in the centre the FNA (twisted out of the normal position) and the VTL; and on the left, the red handles for the loader's firing guard, the BML and the breech closing lever.

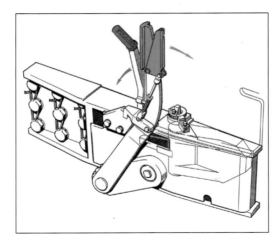

through all angles of elevation – a pressure gauge is located on the left side of the cradle for the loader's use. The other function of the recuperator is to return the gun from fully recoiled to the fully run-out position; this is achieved by the reassertion of the compressed air within the system, which rises to about 1,200psi during recoil. The pistons within the buffers and the recuperator are connected to the gun yoke, which is itself connected to the breech ring and thus transmits the movement of the breech backwards and forwards to the recoil system. Mounted in the 12 o'clock position on the cradle is the replenisher, which is a spring-loaded piston in a cylinder that acts as a reservoir for oil from both buffers; the oil heats up with firing and needs somewhere to go. As the system cools down the spring reasserts on the piston, forcing the cooled oil back into the buffers and replenishing them. On the L11A1 a replenisher was not fitted, leading to recoil problems with a hot gun; this

was rectified with the fitting of the replenisher from the A2 onwards. On the right of the breech ring is the recoil indicator, which is checked by the loader after firing the first round of the day to ensure that the recoil system is functioning correctly and recoil is not excessive.

The coaxial MG mount is part of the cradle to the immediate left of the replenisher cylinder. Behind these two components and in front of the yoke is a square pad, which in full depression contacts a similar pad bolted to the underside of the turret roof; this physically limits the cradle and thus the gun in full depression. Bolted to the left side of the cradle is the semi-automatic cam (SA cam) bracket, which mounts the Breech Mechanism Lever (BML), the Breech Closing Lever and the loader's firing guard. The SA cam is responsible for the semi-automatic opening of the breech – in other words, the breech is initially opened manually by the loader using the BML in order to load the first round, after which the breech opens automatically as part of the run-out sequence following firing, allowing the next round to be loaded – note that for safety reasons the breech does not begin to open until the gun is moving forward.

Firing circuits

In order to fire the MA, there are, at least according to the gunnery handbook, three firing circuits: the normal, the auxiliary and the emergency. The fact is that the auxiliary firing circuit is simply an accident of wiring and serves no real purpose, so we can usefully concentrate on the other two. The function of both circuits

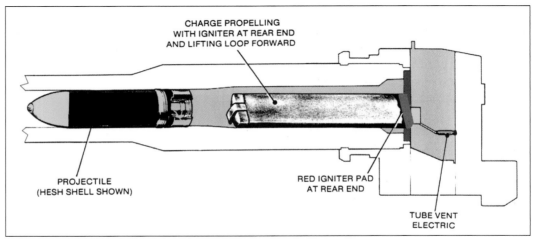

CHARGE PROPELLING WITH IGNITER AT REAR END AND LIFTING LOOP FORWARD

PROJECTILE (HESH SHELL SHOWN)

RED IGNITER PAD AT REAR END

TUBE VENT ELECTRIC

is to deliver an electric current via the Breech Ring Electrical Contact and FNA (both within the breech block) to the base of the VT seated in its chamber in the breech block, thereby igniting the filling and sending a high-energy flash on to the base of the bag-charge via a channel and enlarged flame pocket in the breech block. The cylindrical flame pocket ensures that the flash comes into contact with the whole of the igniter pad at the base of the bagcharge, in turn igniting the propellant which produces the required amount of heat and gas. This pushes the projectile firmly into the rifling causing a gas-tight seal with the driving band, which allows the increasing pressure to force the projectile down the barrel at high speed, being spun by the rifling as it does so.

The battery power required for the main firing circuit comes from the hull batteries; therefore the hull master switch must be ON. In order to activate the circuit, either the gunner (usually) or the commander must select M (Main armament) on their firing handle; the commander's selection on his firing handle will always override the gunner's. Selecting Main will cause the red lamp to illuminate on the Gunner's Fire Control Box to the right of his position. Having already loaded the gun, the loader must pull the movable part of the loader's guard to the rear; this will lock into position and physically prevent him from straying into the path of recoil, and also activate a micro-switch on the safety switch box mounted on the fixed part of the guard. He will ensure that his safety switch is set to Live, completing the firing circuit, and report (shout) 'Loaded!' The gun-ready light on the loader's roof will now be illuminated – this is oriented towards the commander – indicating that the circuit is complete. The gun can now be fired by pressing on one of three firing switches – one each on the commander's and gunner's firing handles, the third is on the elevating handwheel. As he does so, the crewman reports 'Firing now', and, as instructors were fond of regurgitating time and again, pressing the firing switch on the 'ow of now'. All three switches must be checked as part of the routine testing of circuits; for this purpose, a cut-down VT with a pea bulb is used, the bulb illuminating to indicate that the circuit has functioned correctly. (A word of

caution: when on ranges make sure that you are using a circuit tester and not a real VT for this test … it would be embarrassing to get this wrong with the Sqn Gunnery Sergeant standing next to your tank, wouldn't it, Cpl Lomax?)

Should the normal firing circuit fail, part of the misfire drill includes using the emergency firing circuit. At the four o'clock position on the gun cradle adjacent to the gunner's left hip is the Gun Junction Box. This contains a

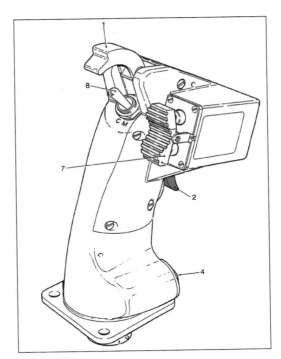

LEFT The firing handle. Both were identical, but the commander's incorporated an override facility which overrode whatever the gunner might have selected. Its main purpose, though, was to allow the commander to fire the guns from his position, the firing switch – never referred to as the trigger – is in red.

BELOW The loader's safety guard: on the left it is shown in the normal open position, thus breaking the firing circuit and making the gun safe. On the right it is in the closed or 'made' position, completing the firing circuit and preventing the loader from straying behind the gun.

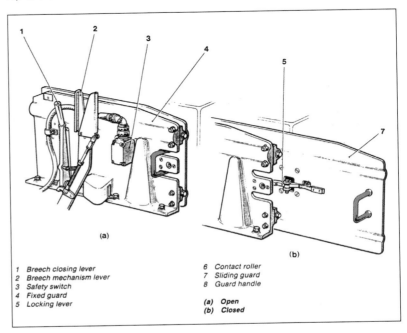

1	Breech closing lever	6	Contact roller
2	Breech mechanism lever	7	Sliding guard
3	Safety switch	8	Guard handle
4	Fixed guard		
5	Locking lever	(a)	Open
		(b)	Closed

small battery and has a two-position switch, marked NORMAL and EMERGENCY. With the switch in the Normal position (rear), the battery is constantly trickle-charged so that it is ready when required. At the rear right of the breech ring is a terminal block with a red push-button firing switch, covered by a protective cap. To use the emergency circuit, the gunner will move the switch forward and report 'Emergency on.' The commander will reach through the cut-out in the shield and remove the protective cap. In a reverse of the usual procedure, the gunner, when the gun is correctly laid on to the target, orders 'Fire.' The commander will then report 'Firing now' and press the button; the crew will continue to use this method until either they can investigate and repair the normal firing circuit, or the emergency battery charge is exhausted. When using the emergency circuit the loader's guard is not part of the circuit, but is still pulled to the rear as a physical safety measure.

Thermal sleeve and fume extractor

When the gun fires, the heat and pressure within the chamber and barrel causes it to heat up rapidly. Imagine then the situation if a thermal sleeve was not fitted: with a hot barrel, a wind blowing from one side would cause the barrel on that side to cool slightly, thus causing the barrel to contract and bend fractionally, which would lead to a loss of accuracy. To prevent this, two fibre thermal blankets or sleeves are wrapped around the barrel, one from the muzzle end to the fume extractor cylinder, and the other to the rear of the cylinder; they are held in place at the ends by screw-threaded clamps and kept together in the centre by a series of straps. Each sleeve is ridged inside to create insulated air pockets. The rearmost portion of the barrel is covered by a corrugated bellows, to allow for the 14in recoil of the MA on firing. When the gun is required to be put into the gun clamp, the pads on the clamp bear against friction pads on the rear of the front sleeve to keep it in place, and a competent crew will regularly retighten it as it can become loose with vibration. (Although the benefits of the thermal sleeve were beyond doubt, production of them could not initially match demand and hence many early vehicles are shown without them.)

The fume extractor is a pressure cylinder mounted around the barrel. It is seated on to two bearing surfaces machined around the barrel, and is efficiently sealed by two toroidal ring seals (and the liberal application of graphite

BELOW The early larger-volume fume extractor; note the early L11 barrel with no MRS shroud on the muzzle.

grease), one at either end, Between the two bearing surfaces are eight gas ports, drilled through the barrel and angled towards the muzzle. When the projectile passes these ports on firing, some of the propellant gases enter the cylinder through the ports and rapidly (milliseconds) build up very high pressure within the cylinder. The instant the projectile leaves the muzzle, the pressure within the barrel drops well below that of the pressure within the cylinder. This causes the gases within the cylinder to equalise, which they do by jetting back through the ports; as these are angled towards the muzzle they create an air flow, forcing the gas and fumes out of the muzzle end. This is assisted by the opening of the breech during run-out, as the clean turret air is dragged through the barrel, helping to scour the last fumes and prevent them from being able to enter the turret. The loader will seal the breech by quickly reloading another projectile, pushing it forwards so that it engages in the rifling. This is advantageous not only in keeping the turret clear of noxious and toxic fumes, but is also a huge advantage if working in a chemical agent vapour environment. A1 and A2 models of the L11 featured a large volume and hence larger fume extractor cylinder; later versions featured a slimline version.

ABOVE The later style of fume extractor. Gun balance counterweights are fitted to the rear (right), and the friction pads for the gun clamp are immediately behind. The weights come in 1lb and 0.5lb sizes, and each gun can be individually balanced with the required number of weights. Note how the front thermal sleeve is fitted over the cylinder and secured with a jubilee clip.

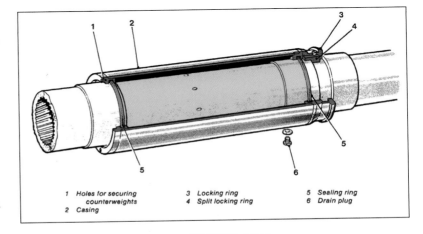

1	Holes for securing	3	Locking ring	5	Sealing ring
	counterweights	4	Split locking ring	6	Drain plug
2	Casing				

ABOVE The internal components of the fume extractor – the cylinder has a small internal volume, in order to build up the maximum pressure inside, which aids efficiency of operation.

LEFT Royal Sovereign of 4RTR has had the front thermal sleeve removed in order to slide the fume extractor forward for servicing: some of the gas ports can be seen. *(Courtesy Keith Paget)*

Cleaning the MA

When the MA has been fired it obviously gets dirty, and it must be kept clean in order to function correctly every time. In particular, the obturators – the sealing rings in the breech that prevent gas escaping into the turret – must be kept immaculately clean. The gunner and the loader, working together as a reasonably well-trained turret crew, will be able to strip, clean and reassemble the MA breech in well under an hour. A really good crew can do this task in 20 minutes. As well as cleaning the breech and its various components, the barrel must also be regularly scrubbed. This is done by assembling a series of wooden and brass staves at the muzzle end of the gun. On the end of these a cleaning brush is attached, which is then liberally doused with engine oil. The crew will then use the staves to vigorously scrub the oily brush up and down the barrel until the bore is clean – a three-man task.

Guns must not be fired when full of oil as this will cause a lot of smoke to be emitted from the muzzle; therefore, once the barrel is clean the same brush is used to pull the barrel through from breech to muzzle, but with an absorbent cotton rag wrapped around it to remove all traces of the oil. The chamber is cleaned from the breech end using a wooden spade grip handle with the special chamber brush, and again scrubbed clean using oil and then dry-cleaned with a rag. With the front thermal sleeve removed, the fume extractor can be unseated and pushed forward towards the muzzle, to allow the fume extractor bearings and the

area between, including the gas ports, to be cleaned and then regreased, making sure that the gas ports are not blocked. With the fume extractor reassembled, the front thermal sleeve is put back into position and all the thermal sleeve clamps retightened. If necessary, the black plastic 'tampon' can be positioned on the muzzle of the gun to prevent the ingress of dirt or sand, and the gun is now ready to be fired again; the tampon is so designed that it can be held in position by an application of grease, but will be pushed off by the increasing forward pressure of the projectile when the next round is fired.

The vision cupola

The No 11 vision cupola fitted to the prototypes was not a success; it had a rotatable binocular sight with a periscope mounted either side giving 164° of vision, and seven fixed periscopes facing to the rear and sides; it was intended to give the commander all-round vision, but it did not do this and the periscopes gave a better view of the sky than the ground. It mounted an M73 .30in MG for the commander's use, and had a split dome hatch, which could be raised up in order to allow the commander to peep over the top of the hatch rim whilst being protected from threats from above, a cause of significant commander casualties in the Second World War. (The earliest design of the cupola proposed a Second World War-style blade vane sight in front, as well as an armoured glass 'arctic wind shield' that rose up when the hatches were raised into the umbrella position.) The gunnery trials found faults with all these areas, and also with the contra-rotation gear designed to speed up target acquisition. As a result, a new No 15 Mk 1 cupola was introduced and trialled on W3 in BAOR in February 1964. This became the standard cupola used on service vehicles, and was itself modified and improved over the years, with the Mk 2 version becoming the standard model, with greater elevation for the commander's MG. The No 40 Mk 1 periscopes used were criticised by the Israelis during their trials; they realised that the tell-tale reflections from the vertical glass faces could be much reduced by

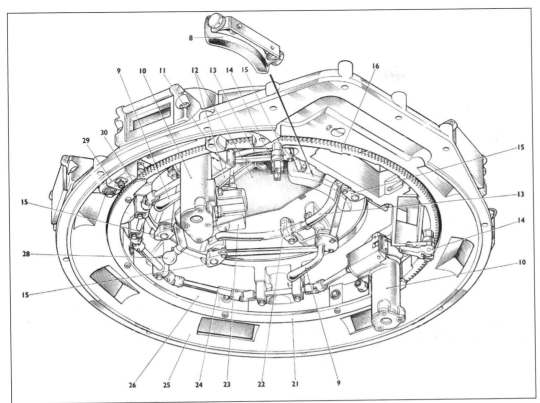

LEFT The No 11 cupola from inside and outside; the design was somewhat archaic and it proved to be an overcomplicated and difficult-to-use item. Its replacement with the No 15 marked a vast improvement in the ability of the commander to observe and engage targets. *(Courtesy M.P. Robinson)*

BELOW A great – and unusual – view of the No 15 cupola, looking up from the loader's floor. This is a pre-IFCS tank but has had Clansman radios installed.

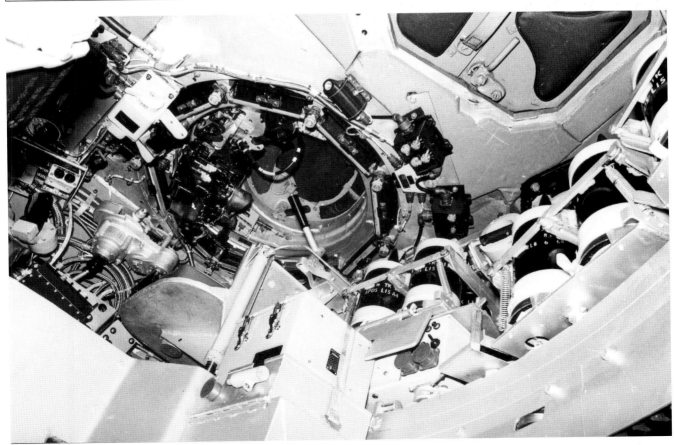

(as later fitted to Khalid), but the tests were
not successful and the GSR was cancelled
in March 1980. The introduction of TOGS in
the late 1980s finally gave the commander a
genuine night-viewing device without the need
to replace the existing cupola.

The RG and laser rangefinder

It was widely realised that the biggest
obstacle to achieving a first-round hit was
not knowing the exact range to the target. If
this could be established, even if the first round
missed the crew could make a correction
and fire again quickly, which would give them
a huge advantage in what was in effect a
quick-draw gunfight. Centurion crews used a
technique whereby if the range was assessed
(*ie* guessed) to be under 1,000yd, the crew
would fire one round of APDS at 800yd, then
another at 1,000yd and a third at 600yd. This
would virtually guarantee that one would hit
due to the flat trajectory and height of the
target – as long as the estimate was not too
far out. Above 1,000yd, a HESH was fired at
a 'best-guesstimated' range to see where it
went, and then the commander would have a
much better idea of the range to the target and
again fire three rounds of APDS at a spread of
three different ranges, for example 1,400, 1,600
and 1,200. Whilst this worked after a fashion,
it was horribly wasteful on ammunition and
did not guarantee a hit, particularly against a
small target. Clearly, things would be improved
massively if the commander could establish an
accurate range before firing.

angling them downwards towards the turret
top. This was done and the item became the
No 40 Mk 2 periscope in British use.

Other cupola types were experimented with,
to try to make target acquisition even faster and
more efficient, and to improve the commander's
night vision capability. GSR 3372 of April
1970 set the requirement for a commander's
combined day/night sight in a cupola with
powered traverse and a thermal pointer. The
No 21 and then No 29 cupolas were designed
and tested, being fitted with the No 84 sight

The concept of an RG, whereby a sub-
calibre weapon is fired to establish the range
before firing a MA round, was British. The
original intention was to use the US-made
lightweight M85 .50 MG as the RG on Chieftain;
this had been developed by GE for the M60
tank. However, it was unable to work with
the higher-pressure British .50 ammunition
required to ballistically match MA ammunition.
Early in 1963, and following other problems
encountered during the gunnery trials, it was
decided that it would be unacceptable for
service use, and the decision was made to
adopt a modified M2 Browning known as the

L21A1, with a special UK-made (Enfield) barrel and a rate-of-fire controller which allowed a burst of three rounds (to improve the likelihood of the gunner observing where they fell) to be fired every time the foot firing pedal was operated, which gave a characteristic 'bop bop bop' sound every time a burst was fired. The M85 was officially cancelled (including the extremely costly US contracts for the gun) in July 1963. The ammunition developed for the L21 had not only a long-burning tracer, but also a flashing tip, respectively designed to aid observation through the air and when it hit something solid. The bursts were fired at a series of pre-determined and increasing ranges; when strikes were observed on target, or burst observed just plus of the target, the range had been established with enough accuracy to fire a MA round. Additionally, the effects of a crosswind observed on the RG ammunition would be applied if firing the slower HESH projectile, again increasing the likelihood of a first-round hit.

RG was first introduced on to a service tank on Centurion; Centurion was also the first tank to use a thermal sleeve system. The use of a RG gave an estimated 20–30% improvement in the chance of a first-round hit using APDS when compared with range estimation; when firing HESH, with its more curving trajectory, the first round was more likely to land in the target area, leading to faster engagements and less wastage of ammunition making corrections. Britain had carried out a convincing demonstration of the efficiency of the RG system using a Centurion in competitive firing trials against an M48, but the US Army was not persuaded. Even the Israelis, who specified a RG *and* a Laser Rangefinder (LRF) in their proposed version of Chieftain, were not totally convinced because they thought that gunners would be unable to spot the RG rounds in the heat of battle, although in their case, the dust of battle is probably more accurate. In British service it was emphasised that the RG was never to be used as an MG, as the special barrels would burn out rapidly if the rate of fire was exceeded.[17] In Chieftain, the RG was mounted to the left side of the 120mm

cradle, and the gun was fitted with a rate-of-fire controller, which limited each burst to the required three rounds. The gunner fired the RG using a foot pedal mounted on his floorplate.

Even as Chieftain was about to enter service with its RG, the army were aware that new technologies might soon be available to replace it, in particular the use of laser technology. Reasonably well understood by 1960, it had been under investigation at the Royal Radar Establishment during the 1950s. In 1964 a requirement was funded for a TLS to be developed (GSR 3187), recognising that the full capacity of the 120mm was being restricted by

---

17 Gunnery purists would *never* refer to it as a Ranging Machine Gun (RMG), but only as the Ranging Gun (RG).

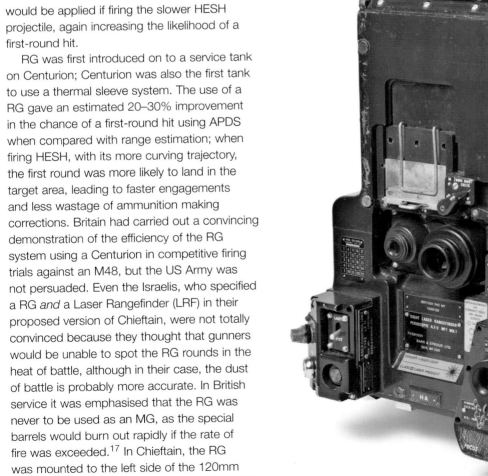

BELOW The TLS No 7 was just one in a series of constantly improving laser sights for the gunner; the left-hand eyepiece was used to provide him with the range readout, whilst the right contained the ballistic graticule pattern and had ×10 magnification. *(TM 8956A2)*

the outdated fire control equipment. The first examples of a laser range-finding sight were made by Barr & Stroud and were ready for trials in 1968, and the promise of such a sight was almost immediately demonstrated. However, it was very unreliable at that stage, and required more years of development before it was ready to enter service in the mid-1970s as the Sight LRF Periscopic No 1 Mk 1, a ruby rod laser system which replaced the existing extended range graticule gunner's sight. This was followed quickly by a whole series of improved sights, all with increased reliability.

When the TLS was fitted, the RG was

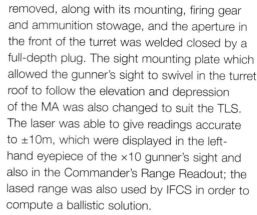

removed, along with its mounting, firing gear and ammunition stowage, and the aperture in the front of the turret was welded closed by a full-depth plug. The sight mounting plate which allowed the gunner's sight to swivel in the turret roof to follow the elevation and depression of the MA was also changed to suit the TLS. The laser was able to give readings accurate to ±10m, which were displayed in the left-hand eyepiece of the ×10 gunner's sight and also in the Commander's Range Readout; the lased range was also used by IFCS in order to compute a ballistic solution.

The same GSR 3187 also required the fitting of a commander's firing station, to allow the commander to monitor and, if necessary, fire the armaments from his position, an innovative request. Although it was always appreciated that some accuracy would be lost when the commander fired the gun, due to the complicated mechanical linkages required, it was a sensible enhancement and its introduction was appreciated by the crews; when IFCS was introduced an updated version was fitted with a firing handle to the same design as the gunner's, but with an override facility.

Fire control system improvements

The use of a Muzzle Boresight (MBS) was suggested by RSM (I) Robinson RTR of the Gunnery School and then developed into service by Maj (Retd) C.J. Wieland, ex-RTR and serving at FVRDE; Wieland was also central in developing the later MRS. The use of a boresight recognised the tendency of a long barrel to droop at the muzzle due to its own weight, so-called girder stress. This meant that an optical instrument which defined the axis of the bore at the muzzle end was inherently more accurate than the previous method of looking down the whole length of the bore from the breech end using binoculars. The ×7 MBS allowed the gunner to accurately align his sights (main and auxiliary) with the axis of the bore at a range of 1,000m; the commander could also adjust his Projector Reticle Image (PRI), which injected a copy of the gunner's graticule pattern into his sight at the same time.

This innovation was not the complete answer

ABOVE Crews of B Sqn 3RTR boresight their guns at Castlemartin ranges, 1979; the case for the sight is lying on the ground with the cover open … shame on you Cpl Treffry! *(Courtesy Andrew Chapman)*

LEFT A close-up of the Boresight No 6, a critical piece of equipment used when setting the sights up. *(TM 10666.001, 002)*

to shooting accurately though. It had been proved that a Centurion armed with a perfectly zeroed 20-pounder would, after two hours of steady firing, have lost accuracy equivalent to missing the point of aim by about 1.5m at 1,000m; it was clear that a method was needed to ensure that the initial accuracy imparted by the boresight could be maintained during firing. Thus the same GSR (3187) that had specified the LRF in 1964 also specified the installation of a system that would maintain gun/sight relationship during firing. This led to the development of the MRS, which began in 1969, using Chieftain 03SP01. In essence, MRS worked like this: once sight adjustment had been completed using the MBS as described above, a light source mounted on the turret roof was switched on, shining a circular red light on to a polished steel mirror mounted on the muzzle. The red disc of light was reflected back into the gunner's sight, and then adjusted so that it filled the circle (the MBS mark) at the top centre of the gunner's graticule pattern. Once locked in this position, it was not affected by firing in the same way that the gunner's sight was, and so provided a constant reference point that did not move around during firing. Having fired a few rounds, generally during a lull at the end of an engagement, the gunner

LEFT The SU No 70, aka emergency telescope, in use by a budding troop leader on his course at Lulworth. (It was obligatory to pull a face whilst using it …) *(TM 10059-002)*

LEFT The MRS mirror was a highly polished steel bar dowelled on to a 'forged upstand', a flat platform on the top of the muzzle. The mirror was protected from damage by a distinctive rubber shroud, which also provided a dark non-reflective area for the mirror to work within.

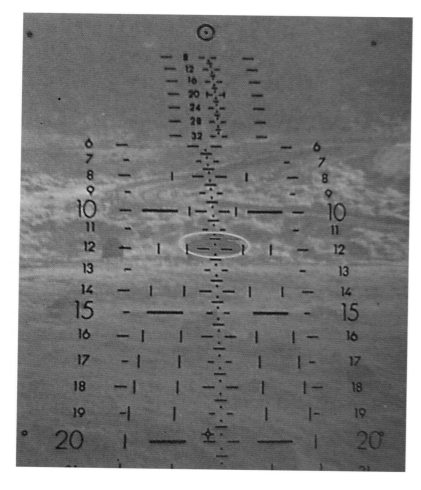

would quickly check that the red disc was still coincident within the MBS mark. If it was, gun/sight alignment was correct. If not, he simply adjusted the graticule pattern until coincidence was regained. The whole procedure of checking and adjusting took only a few seconds, and represented a major advance in maintaining accuracy, even after firing many rounds. (Neither the Sight Unit (SU) nor the PRI could be used with MRS, but once the gunner had realigned the TLS using MRS, he could quickly lay on to a clearly defined object at 1,000m and adjust his SU, whilst the commander realigned the PRI.)

IFCS

GSR 3540 of 1 June 1970 ordered the development of a ballistic computer-based fire control system, which would speed up the engagement sequence, increase the range at which the 120mm could be used and improve the chances of hitting a moving target. This led to the development of the IFCS, which followed hot on the heels of the introduction of TLS and entered service around 1980; Mks 5–8 retrofitted with IFCS all became Mk 9s.

LEFT An example of the early graticule pattern used on IFCS tanks – the MBS red light had to fit snugly within the circle at the top centre. Note the ellipse aiming mark generated at 1,200m on the HESH scale.

RIGHT A common sight for the crews but less often caught on camera – the IFCS Computer and Interface Unit (CIU) on top of the turret of this 1RTR Mk 11 named Dauphine. Its in-use position was underneath the gunner's seat.

As well as using the lased range information from the TLS, IFCS used a number of other sensors mounted around the tank to take into account factors that affected the chances of a hit – wind speed, air temperature and pressure, bag-charge temperature and amount of wear in the barrel, to name a few. As well as converting the tanks, nearly 800 in all, all crews had to undergo conversion courses in the regiments to allow them to understand the new and complex system, and practise the multitude of engagement routines and techniques that the new system demanded. (For a description of the system operation, see the Haynes Manual *Challenger 1 Main Battle Tank*, pages 77–78.)

MBSGD

Multi-Barrelled Smoke Grenade Dischargers (MBSGDs) were a feature on most British Armoured Fighting Vehicles (AFVs) by the 1950s, and gave the crew the means to fire a rapid defensive smokescreen around their vehicle in order to get out of trouble. On Chieftain, the prototypes started by mounting six individual tubes each side of the turret, developed from those used on Centurion and Conqueror. Later, the prototypes and Mk 1 tanks featured a new design, a pair of cast six-barrelled dischargers either side of the turret, with a number of different mounting positions being experimented with. A close inspection will show two different styles in use, both similar but with subtle differences. The early model (No 7) used on the Mk 1 was found to produce an uneven spread of grenades, leading to gaps appearing in the screen. As a result, a revised type (the No 9) was introduced in 1965 on the Mk 2 onwards, which solved the problem and gave a lateral spread of 1,812mils (about 102°) when firing all 12 L5, L7 or L8 grenades simultaneously. The latter type was WP, which burst in the air and produced an almost instantaneous screen

BELOW Very few IFCS tanks were fitted with a meteorological probe, mounted on the turret roof. This provided the computer with accurate information on local wind speed and direction, air temperature and pressure. The tank in a squadron with the probe could pass the information to the remainder, allowing the commanders to input manually the readings into their own systems.

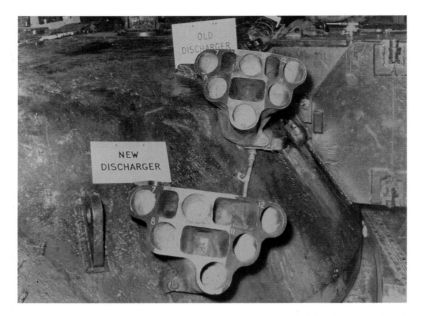

ABOVE **The design differences between the No 7 (old) and No 9 (new) MBSGDs were quite subtle but can be compared here.**

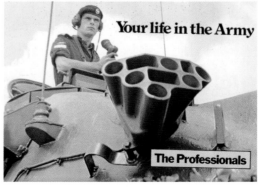

ABOVE AND RIGHT
The early No 7 MBSGD on prototype and Mk 1 vehicles (above) and the revised No 9 pattern used on all other marks (right).
(Courtesy Andy Brend)

that lasted about 60 seconds, whereas the first two burned for about 30 seconds longer but landed on the ground and took a few seconds to build up. When not loaded, the dischargers were protected by canvas covers to keep the barrels clean and dry.

NBC protection

The prototype vehicles were not originally fitted with an NBC/ventilation pack, although the intention was always to fit them on to the service vehicles, as the primary environment that Chieftain was expected to operate in was a nuclear and chemical war. First trialled on prototypes P3 and P5 in early 1964 and fitted from PP1 through to most Mk 3s, the No 2 Mk 1 pack was the first such system in service. It was a relatively simple system: with all the hatches closed, air was drawn through a pre-filter and then a main particulate filter housed in an armoured box on the turret right rear, and the clean air was then distributed to the crew positions, either collectively or via ducting to which each crewman could, if necessary, fit his respirator using flexible rubber hoses. By producing an overpressure, whereby the pressure inside the fighting compartment was greater than that outside, air would always travel from the inside of the tank towards the outside, thereby preventing the ingress of contamination. Excess overpressured air was allowed to escape using a Pressure Relief Valve (PRV) mounted under a small armoured cover immediately behind the commander's cupola. When just ventilation was selected (by the loader using a control box mounted to the left-hand turret wall), the air would only come through the pre-filter before being passed around the tank; although it was often nice to have cool air being blown into the inside, it was not the same as air conditioning on a hot day. (When it was hot outside, it was always hotter inside the tank, and when it was cold outside, it was always colder inside …)

From the Mk 3/3 on, the more sophisticated No 6 Mk 1 pack made by Microflow Ltd of Farnborough was fitted during production, employing four stages of filtration, giving even cleaner air. The No 6 pack was in a larger armoured box, fitting

RIGHT The original No 2 NBC pack armoured cover on a Mk 1 tank; air was drawn in and filtered, and then distributed into the tank via the armoured ducting to the left. Access to the main filter was from the underside. The cowl on the top was originally to cool the fan motor, but on Mk 3 vehicles the design was altered so it became the air intake.

BELOW The air flow from the No 6 NBC pack. The blue arrows show the main routes through which overpressured air escapes outwards, preventing chemical agents or radiological contamination from entering the crew compartment.

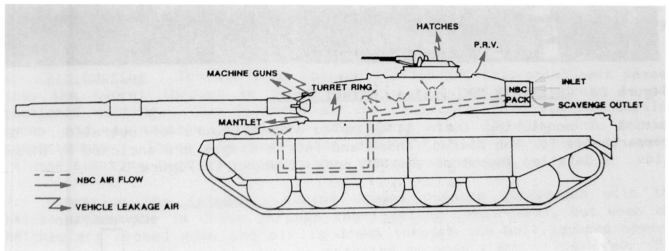

across the whole width of the turret rear, and accessed by a large hinged door; the pack door had to be opened in order to change the 120mm gun barrel through the turret rear. The Mk 5 MBT used the No 6 Mk 2, which differed only in that it did not have a pre-filter bypass facility. During the Totem Pole programme of upgrades, all Mk 2 to 3/3 tanks had the No 6 Mk 2 pack fitted. Towards the end of its service life, many Chieftains were fitted with the No 11 pack. Externally identical to the No 6, the pack featured two large cylindrical high-efficiency filters and a push-button No 15 digital control box in the loader's side.

Despite all this sophistication, crewmen were still expected to operate wearing their protective

LEFT The No 6 NBC pack door open, with the filter compartments inside. The square panel now revealed in the turret rear centre would be unbolted to allow the gun barrel, which weighed 1,073kg, to be changed.

NBC suits, with respirators ready at hand; if collective protection was breached, crews would need to be able to 'fight dirty' – wearing the full ensemble including overboots and gloves. Training in BAOR (and in British Army Training Unit Suffield (BATUS)) majored on this area in the 1970s and '80s, and it was a rare exercise when NBC suits were not required to be worn most of the time.

IR equipment

From the outset, it was intended to equip Chieftain with the most modern night-fighting equipment available; in the 1960s this meant the use of equipment working in the IR part of the electromagnetic spectrum that had been developed in the previous decade and was now mature enough for service use. For fighting, the turret mounted a white-light and IR-Light Projector on the LHS, and both the gunner and commander were able to swap their normal day sights for IR sights. The gunner's sight was the

RIGHT Exercises wearing NBC suits and respirators were tiring, as this commander proves. Note the L42 binoculars. The ammunition box carrier is fitted on to the side of the MG mounting; a later type had a tray for the box on the cupola ...

RIGHT ... as demonstrated admirably by the author's photograph of his own cupola on exercise. Note the camouflaged RAC steel helmet, conveniently stowed and protecting the spotlight. The butt for the L37 GPMG is ready to hand, taped to the top of the sight mount, and the pig mascot came from a German butcher's.

ABOVE The IR gunner's sight was fitted at night in place of the normal day sight, and used in conjunction with the Light Projector and its IR filter. It was limited in range and was infrequently used, before being rendered redundant by the introduction of TOGS.

HEAD ASSEMBLY

EYEPIECE FOCUSSING KNOB

GRATICULE ADJUSTING KNOB / HORIZONTAL

SPARE HEAD ASSEMBLY (SHUTTER OPEN)

DO NOT OPERATE IN DAYLIGHT WITH SHUTTERS OPEN

LOCKING LEVERS

SHUTTER CONTROL LEVER

ILLUMINATOR UNIT KNOB

GRATICULE ADJUSTING KNOB / VERTICAL

×3 magnification No 33, which had a simplified graticule pattern with a range of 1,700m and which replaced his ×8 day sight; the commander used IR binoculars No 7 to replace the prismatic binoculars on the No 11 cupola. The No 15 cupola mounted a spotlight with an IR filter, and the driver also had an IR swap sight, used in conjunction with IR driving lights.

In October 1967, the RAC Equipment Trials Wing (ETW) began tests on an image intensifier (II) swap sight for the driver. The II works by amplifying minute amounts of ambient light, and has the advantage of being a passive system; development of the sight led to the IR driver's periscope being replaced with the first of a number of II versions around 1974. The sights could be swapped over in a couple of minutes, with the one not in use stowed within the driver's compartment. Crews discovered that the vision improved if the IR headlamps were switched on, which negated the passivity of the II sight but made for a better drive.

ABOVE Using the night sight in strong light could damage the instrument, so shutters were provided to allow the sight to be boresighted to the gun during daylight.

LEFT B Sqn QRIH on exercise in Germany, 1973. The commander's spotlight (here fitted with the removable IR filter) could be moved by traversing the cupola, and elevated or depressed with the same controls used for the commander's MG. Note the IR detector stalk fitted behind the cupola. (Courtesy Jonathan Falconer)

ABOVE The No 2, used on the prototypes, employed an 18in reflector to give the maximum range and usable beam. The centre-hinged doors were unsuccessful and the armoured box was far too heavy, which led to a redesign.

ABOVE White light being used during the day on an exercise to represent the 120mm firing – when the projector was switched on and the cover opened, the IR filter was in place. If the commander then selected white light the filter would open, giving 2kW of white light, which could be boosted to 3kW for up to ten seconds at a time.

BELOW A Mk 2 showing the external IR components fitted; the IR filters on the headlights would be replaced by the two smaller pairs of headlights from Mk 3 production onwards. Note the anti-slip matting on the hull bins and turret roof.

(COMMANDER'S) SPOTLIGHT No. 2 MK 1

RECEIVER INFRA - RED DETECTING SET, L1A1

PERISCOPE, A.V. L1A1 (COMMANDER'S)

LIGHT PROJECTOR No. 2 MK 3

GHT, PERISCOPE, A.V. L1A1 (GUNNER'S)

HEADLIGHT IR FILTER

03 EB 35

PERISCOPE, A.V. L2A1 (DRIVER'S)

The Light Projector (commonly called the searchlight) mounted to the left side of the turret began life as the No 2 with an 18in reflector and a white-light xenon lamp which could be used with an IR filter to provide IR light; however, one of the problems acknowledged with IR was that an enemy equipped with similar equipment would be easily able to see both the beams and the vehicles producing them. For that reason this was known as an active system. The first design featured split doors hinged in the centre, was welded directly to the turret and was armoured with 17mm plate. This added around 250kg at a time when the tank was already too heavy and was also very expensive, so the final design, the 19in No 2 Mk 3, featured a removable mounting in one-eighth-inch mild steel instead, along with a single side-hinged door. The box was designed not to protrude over the hull side (for railway transportation), and also to allow the driver to escape should it be positioned above his hatch. It had two power settings: 2kW was normal, and it could be boosted by the commander to 3kW for no more than ten seconds at a time.

An IR detection system was fitted to give the commander warning that he had been 'illuminated' by an enemy using IR. This consisted of a 25.5in-high stalk that fitted on to a socket on the turret roof behind the cupola, with a control box on the left of the commander's position. If an active IR source illuminated one – or more – of the three cells in the stalk, an audible alarm would sound, and a lamp on the control unit would illuminate. By operating each of the three push-button switches on the control unit in turn, the commander could work out roughly where the threat was in relation to his turret.

Navigation Set Land Vehicular

Navigation Set Land Vehicular (NAVAID) was an inertial navigation system that was fitted on early marks of Chieftain, and seems to have been regularly used in the early days; it was often referred to positively in accounts in regimental journals. However, for unknown reasons it fell out of favour and by the time the author was first trained on the tank in 1977 it was not even mentioned. There must

have been a good reason for this because, on the face of it, it was a winner, providing the commander with an eight-figure grid reference (equivalent to an accuracy of 10m), and both the commander and driver with a heading/bearing indicator. The main components were mounted behind the driver's position: a gyro compass, a power supply unit and the control box. The system computer was mounted above the gearbox controller in the cab, and

ABOVE AND BELOW The IR detection equipment was a good idea in theory but fiddly to use in practice. Some crews claimed that it could be used as an alarm clock, by setting the sensitivity control to cause the alarm to go off at daybreak.

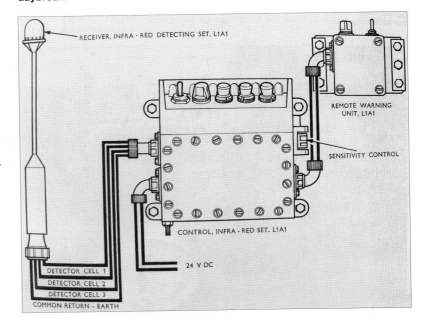

ABOVE Firing now! D Sqn 4RTR firing at BATUS; many commanders found navigation the greatest challenge on these exercises. *(Courtesy David Moffat)*

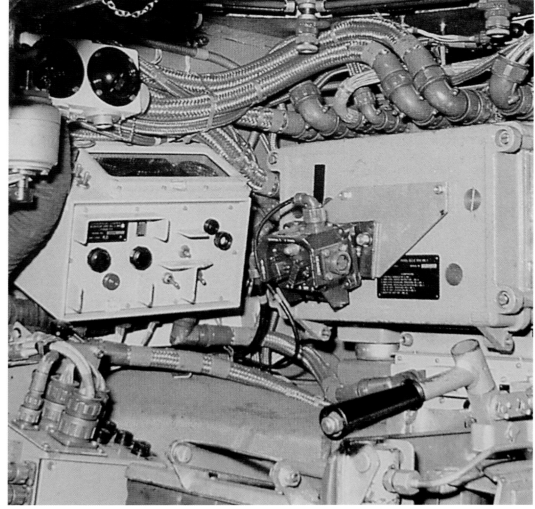

RIGHT An unusual combination – by the time that IFCS was introduced in the early 1980s, almost all Chieftains had been fitted with Clansman radios and harness. This IFCS tank, with the Commander's Control and Monitoring Unit (CCMU) declaring its status, still has the Larkspur radio system fitted, with the commander's box mounted behind his seat.

the commander had a control and display unit mounted on the turret roof to his rear left – not exactly convenient but there was nowhere else it could be fitted. Distance travelled was input from the vehicle speedometer into the computer, and inertial dead-reckoning from a known start point gave the position. On the very first MEDICINE MAN exercise on the desert-like prairies of Canada, 4RTR recorded: 'We discovered a new and valuable friend in the much maligned NAVAID, especially when we did a night march over featureless ground and ended up in exactly the right place. [The three tanks that had the equipment] were much envied by the remainder. The squadron leader was often heard on the radio asking his second in command who had NAVAID "Where the hell are we?"'

Radio systems

When first produced, Chieftain was equipped with the recently introduced Larkspur radio system, comprising (in gun tanks) a C42 radio for squadron use, and a smaller B47 for use on the troop net. Although reasonable, its days were numbered by the mid-1970s with the impending introduction of the replacement system, Clansman. This was a much more modern and easier to use system, complete with dial-up frequencies and simplified antenna tuning. A range of new audio equipment was provided for the crew, and the Live Intercommunication (IC) facility – allowing all crew members to communicate with each other without having to press a switch – was hailed as a major advance. Clansman conversion was originally intended to be complete by 1973, but the usual difficulties in developing the system meant that it only commenced in mid-1978, and by the early 1980s almost every vehicle had been converted, save some of the driver training tanks in the UK. A story of the time – the author cannot vouch for its authenticity – had it that the 353 radio could have been made much smaller than it was, saving valuable space in the turret. However, the specification was poorly worded and had stated the external dimensions as those to be achieved, rather than what was intended – which was the maximum that the set should be. …

1 B47 radio set B	8 Boiling vessel sockets
2 C42 radio set	9 Boiling vessel socket switch
3 Ammunition stowage	10 Circuit breaker C1
4 Circuit breaker C4	11 Fuse cover
5 Circuit breaker C3	12 Overriding master control
6 Boiling vessel socket	switch handle
switch	13 Circuit breaker C5
7 Circuit breaker C6	14 Circuit breaker C2
	15 Drinking water

LEFT The Larkspur radio installation, with the larger C42 radio on the right (2), and the smaller B47 in the tunnel (1). When Clansman was introduced, two Vehicle Radio Communications (VRC) 353 radios could be fitted where the C42 used to be, and so more projectiles were stowed in the tunnel.

LEFT Cpl Phil May of B Sqn 3RTR (at the time the author's tank commander) wearing the Clansman staff user headsets and Commander's Pressel Unit (CPU) in 1980. The boom microphone and Live IC was a real advance in crew efficiency. By the late 1980s, berets were banned from use on AFVs, and the crewman's helmet had to be worn – officially at least.

Chapter Four

Chieftain in service

Over 1,000 Chieftain MBTs and variants saw service in the British Army over a 30-year period. Following the success of Centurion, there were great hopes that Chieftain would achieve large sales in export markets, and eventually nearly 1,500 more vehicles served in foreign armies.

OPPOSITE Cpl Andy Fisher of 3RTR ready to load a 120mm HESH projectile into the gun. He is wearing the Mk 3 NBC suit and Clansman staff user headsets, the latter sometimes impeding the efficient (fast) loading of the gun but necessary, as the loader was also the radio operator. *(Courtesy Andrew Chapman)*

ABOVE A busy (posed)
tank park scene at the
Central Vehicle Depot,
Ludgershall – Mk 2
02EB48 is checked
and prepared by the
REME ready for issue.
(TM 7238E3)

took place before this could happen, so the third regiment equipped became 2RTR. The Prime Minister Harold Wilson even became involved in the fielding plan and, in a style reminiscent of Churchill, ordered that the first two Chieftains had to be in service in BAOR by 30 September 1965; in the event, he had no more success than the professionals involved, and the target date was missed by over a year. Having undertaken extensive training courses at the RAC Centre during 1966, the 11th Hussars received their first six tanks on 11 November 1966, with bulk issues starting in January 1967 so that the whole regiment was equipped by 24 March of the same year. There followed a punishing but interesting series of user trials and exercises, made even more complicated by the necessity for the tanks to be constantly modified, and for prying eyes (meaning the Warsaw Pact) to be kept away from the tanks. By the time the next regiment (17/21L) were fully equipped in January 1968, the Hussars' tanks had all completed between 800 and 1,150 miles each, totalling 28,000 miles in under a year – not bad for an unreliable tank. Once under way, production continued at a good pace, so that the sixth regiment, 14th/20th King's Hussars (14/20H), received all their tanks by May 1969.

Entering service

The problems with development and trials – and particularly the engine – covered in Chapters One and Two – meant that the originally intended in-service date (ISD) of April 1962 was never going to be met. Based on that date, the original fielding order for the new tanks was to be 11th Hussars, 17th/21st Lancers (17/21L) and then 3RTR. However, the many delays meant that regimental rotations

RIGHT Mk 2 02EB44
is signed for by its
new owners, as it is
loaded on to an Antar
tank transporter – the
crates on the engine
decks contain the
tools. This tank ended
up as a hard target on
Lulworth ranges.
(TM 7238E1)

The CO of the 11th Hussars, Lt Col Peter Hamer OBE, produced an extremely insightful report detailing the tank's entry into service, key points from which are reproduced here:

Performance. This has exceeded all expectations. Road speed is a genuine 30mph. Cross country performance is greatly improved, and a much smoother ride than Centurion is given. On a regimental move 20 miles can be maintained in the hour with no trouble. Oil consumption on all vehicles is high, however it does diminish as the mileage of vehicles increases. Engine smoke is considerable. The tank is very cold and dirty.

120mm gun. The performance of this gun has astounded everyone.

Stowage. There is not enough stowage space. Some 20 baskets from the rear of old Conqueror turrets have been acquired and with little modification fit on the back of the turret.

Conclusion. This is a first-class tank which deserves to get large overseas sales orders.

In the period between 11 November 1966 and 1 November 1967, only six powerpacks had been changed (only one of which was classified as a serious fault), along with five GUEs and two TN12 gearboxes, one of which was put down to 'serious bad driving'. The report also noted how easy the tank was to drive, candidly recording that 'The Commanding Officer's fourteen year old son could handle the tank very adequately in about 15 minutes.' Clearly he and his crews were impressed, although they were not blind to some of the tank's shortcomings. At about the same time, a diligent RAC staff officer listed Chieftain's advantages over Centurion; he also listed Chieftain's disadvantages compared to Centurion, an interesting list, which read:

- Complicated main gun;
- Less ammunition;
- Poorer rear hull protection;
- Slower barrel change;
- Dirtier, colder, noisier.

Chieftain certainly was a very dirty, cold and noisy tank, as all crewmen who served on her will testify; in fact, when he spoke at the RAC Conference of 1967, Hamer's final words were

LEFT Cold! Chieftain could be a miserable tank to work on, always dirty and oily, with smelly diesel fuel. What was even worse was that work often had to be done in extremes of weather. A leaguer of 3RTR vehicles in BATUS, where the MEDICINE MAN 7 exercise, the final one of the season, was often conducted in near-arctic conditions. *(Courtesy Andrew Chapman)*

a plea from the heart on behalf of his crews: 'Please may we have heaters?' And Colonel Hamer's final comment above regarding the potential for export sales is important: Centurion had brought large amounts of export money into the economy, and kept tank production factories (and their subcontractors) in work. It was hoped – and believed – that Chieftain might do the same; exporting tanks also allowed some of the considerable costs of research and development to be paid for elsewhere. However, the export drives were much less successful than hoped for, and we will in due course examine who the tank was offered to, who wanted to purchase the tank, and who actually received Chieftains; they were not the same. ...

BAOR and BATUS: three decades of rehearsals

In retrospect, we can be thankful that Chieftain was never called upon to prove its virtues as an MBT on the battlefield of north-west Europe, but it did of course see combat in the Iran–Iraq War, as well as during the Iraqi invasion of Kuwait in 1990 – these aspects will be mentioned in due course. The only time Chieftain went to war with the British Army was as Royal Engineer (RE) variants, used in the liberation of Kuwait in 1991.

As previously noted, life for the Chieftain crewman was a fairly hard affair, and as the tank became more complicated as more systems were added, the amount of time spent on the 'tank park' just conducting routine servicing took a considerable time. As a rule, before the tank was used for the first time each day, the 'first parade' checks had to be carried out to make sure that both engines had sufficient oil, the coolant level was correct, and visually there were no leaks or obvious faults. When the tank was in use a series of regular 'halt parades' were conducted to identify any potential problems before they became serious; for example, the driver would place the back of his hand against each wheel hub in turn, to check for signs of overheating. And as the tank was shut down at the end of each day, the 'last parade' checks were carried out, again topping up levels (if safe to do so) and rectifying faults.

ABOVE A typical mid-exercise scene in Germany c.1984: 3RTR tanks in a regimental leaguer during an FTX, a non-tactical formation allowing administration and maintenance between phases.

RIGHT FTX in BAOR could involve movement over large parts of northern Germany. This is the author's map – prior to being cut down into more manageable pieces – on one such exercise.

In good units, each crew member noted faults that he could not immediately rectify in a notebook, in order to report them to the commander for subsequent action. And this was just the routine side; repairing faults, changing brake pads, bleeding the steering hydraulics, knocking out dust from the air filters, cleaning leaves and debris from the radiator matrix, these and a hundred other time-consuming but necessary actions were undertaken by the crew to keep the tank in good order. The gunner would likewise be responsible for cleaning the MGs (three when the RG was fitted) and carrying out the six- and eight-point functional checks on them, maintaining the batteries, servicing the recoil system, checking firing circuits, and scrubbing

RIGHT Chieftain crews wearing NBC suits – which kept them warm in the winter, but were hot and uncomfortable the rest of the year.

ABOVE A lot of time was spent camouflaged under netting deep in German woods, more to avoid being spotted from the air than to protect from ground observation. *(Courtesy Andrew Chapman)*

RIGHT Now you see it – now you don't. Camouflage was close to being an obsession amongst tank crews in BAOR, as it was understood as being an important part of staying alive on the battlefield. Here a crew demonstrate the use of painted hessian – bulky to carry but incredibly effective in the right setting.

the barrel and breech of the MA. One of the advantages of this regular contact with the tank – although it may not have been seen like this at the time – was that the crews, and their REME counterparts, became really experts on the tank, and were thus often able to stop faults before they became serious,

and repair the tank and keep it 'on the road'. (A tank in an inoperative condition was known as VOR – Vehicle Off Road.) Other armies practised different philosophies of supporting their tanks, including many who preferred to have separate maintenance crews, almost in the manner of an F1 team. However, despite the extra workload, the crews of Chieftain all agreed that their training was the best – a strong bond between them and the Chieftain as a tank developed, despite its many foibles and faults, and particularly with the individual tank that they crewed. No one enjoyed working on someone else's tank; it was never quite the same as being on their own; almost everyone believed that 'their' tank was the best in the army. It was official

LEFT Refuelling from a Stalwart-mounted UBRE, or Unit Bulk Refuelling Equipment. This was so much quicker and wasted less fuel through spillage than the alternative method of filling by jerrycans. *(Courtesy David Moffat)*

LEFT A Stillbrew-
equipped 'enemy'
Mk 10 on an FTX in
Germany, with an
umpire Landrover
in the background.
Fitting camouflage
netting around the
barrel to break up
its long shape was
common practice.
(Courtesy Carl Schulze)

policy to reduce the movement of crewmen
between tanks to the minimum, so that the
crews would get to know each other and their
particular tank intimately.

As well as this constant contact with the
tank, formal training took place using the
suite of training aids and simulators that were
provided, of which more in due course. Training
included the initial training courses to qualify
crewmen, commanders and instructors, and
then constant refresher training in both the
technical and tactical aspects of the role.
Each unit in Germany would undergo a regular
training cycle, including an intensive refresher
training period followed immediately by the
annual two-week live-firing gunnery camp,
usually on the Bergen-Hohne ranges, as well

ABOVE Another
'enemy' tank, this time
a Mk 11, using orange
minetape to
announce its identity.
(Courtesy Carl Schulze)

LEFT A Mk 10 of
14/20H in the Berlin
urban camouflage
scheme looks out
of place in a
woodland setting.
(Courtesy Carl Schulze)

as between four to twelve weeks spent in the field on tactical training exercises. These started on the SLTA and progressed on to exercises over the German countryside, known as FTX. Additionally, each armoured squadron could expect to visit BATUS in Canada on average once every two years, which, from 1972, allowed much more realistic and demanding

LEFT A patchy snow camouflage was adopted by 3RTR during this winter exercise in Germany. The temporary white camouflage was not paint, but was supplied as a dry powder which was mixed with solvent, and applied with brushes, soft brooms or even rags.

BRITISH ARMY POST-PRODUCTION AND NON-STANDARD MARKS

Mk	Automotive	Turret and firepower	Equipment code	Remarks
1/1	Mk 1/2 automotive standard; IR headlamps; oil-lubricated top rollers; improved air cleaner; improved exhaust and rear hull.	Nil change	0300-2011	Becomes Mk 1/1 (Y) after Y Totem Pole mods incorporated.
1/2	Mk 1/2 automotive standard; IR headlamps; oil-lubricated top rollers; improved air cleaner; improved exhaust and rear hull.	No 15 Mk 1 cupola; No 9 MBSGD.	0300-2012	REME conversion. Becomes Mk 1/2 (Y) after Y Totem Pole mods incorporated.
1/3	Mk 1/1 with XYZ Totem Pole mods incorporated.		0300-2013	
1/4	Mk 1/2 with XYZ Totem Pole mods incorporated. Used for conversion to AVLB.		0300-2014	
6	Mk 2 with XYZ Totem Pole mods incorporated.		0300-2060	
7	Mks 3, 3/G, 3/2, 3/S with XYZ Totem Pole mods incorporated.		0300-2070	
8	Mks 3/3 with XYZ Totem Pole mods incorporated.		0300-2080	
9	Nil	IFCS; full APFSDS stowage.	0300-2090	Modified from Mk 5, 6, 7 or 8. Mk 9 had three Phases but only Phase 1 was fully implemented across the fleet, making it difficult to track the exact modification state of Mk 9 tanks.
10	L60 Mk 13A. H30 Mk 7A or 10A. TN12 Mk 4.	Stillbrew, No 11 NBC pack, GCE No 10.	0300-3093	Modified from Mk 9. Not all vehicles received the new NBC pack.
11	Nil	TOGS	0300-3094	Modified from Mk 10. Not all Mk 10s were modified.

Notes:
Many of the improvements and modifications listed were incorporated at different times; it was only when all the major modifications had been embodied that the mark and equipment code of the tank were amended.
On completion of Clansman radio installation, the suffix C was added to the mark.
Marks 12, 13 and 14 were planned but not implemented, hence Omani vehicles being called Mk 15.

training to be conducted, including a lot of Fire and Movement Exercises (FMX), in which tactical movement was incorporated with live firing, something that could not be easily done in Europe due to safety limitations.

It is probably fair to say that almost every tank crewman in Germany – and the supporting personnel – was very well trained and would be expected to acquit themselves well in the event of war. Due to the overwhelming superiority of the Warsaw Pact forces on the other side of the IGB – the Inner German Border – any conflict could be expected to be hard and bloody, so the prospects of it were taken seriously. Thus it was essential to keep the Chieftains in tip-

ABOVE On the tank park in BATUS, as crews prepare for Exercise MEDICINE MAN – a REME 434 is lifting a TN12 gearbox, an all too common sight.

LEFT A typical BATUS tank, probably a Mk 6 to 8. The white lines on the turret roof are known as 'forty-fives', and are used by the commander as a safety aid. If he has been given permission by the safety staff to open fire, and no one is within the forty-fives, he can fire. *(Courtesy Andrew Chapman)*

LEFT Washing down was a necessary task after each exercise period, in order to remove the mud before conducting post-mission servicing. *(Courtesy Fraser Gray)*

RIGHT A still-wet Mk 11 of 4RTR named Diplodocus straight after going through the washdown. Once dry, the tank would be streaked with remnants of mud and dirt. The tracks could do with a bit of tightening.

THE STORY OF A TANK

BELOW AND BELOW RIGHT Tank 04EB49 in its heyday, as the OC's tank of B Sqn 4RTR in Munster in the early 1980s, before being used as a range target at Lulworth.

Let us look at the life and times of a typical Chieftain MBT, to get an idea of the sort of service that one tank might undertake. The tank in question is 04EB49, built as a Mk 2 by Leeds, which entered service in April 1969, but did not immediately go to a regiment, but into storage as part of the War Maintenance Reserve (WMR). It only started its active career with 2RTR in Munster, Germany, in 1972, and left there to be upgraded in June 1975. It was then held in storage by 2 Armour Delivery Squadron (ADS) in Hamm from October 1975 until February the following year, when it went to 4RTR in Munster. It was then upgraded again in March 1976, and returned to storage with 2ADS between December 1978 and February 1979. It then went back to 4RTR

and was upgraded for the third time in May 1979. It was then taken over by Queen's Royal Irish Hussars (QRIH) in July 1982, before going to 2ADS again in August 1983. It was received by 2RTR for the second time in Fallingbostel in January 1984, and it was given its fourth upgrade in September, before being handed over to 1RTR in Hildesheim in December 1984. The fifth and sixth upgrades followed in November 1985 and April 1986, before returning to 2ADS in April 1989. It was held as a reserve before being Struck off Strength in February 1999, and was then sent, after 30 years spent in Germany, to Lulworth, to be used as a range target; at the end of its life the photograph shows that it has Stillbrew armour fitted and thus was either a Mk 10 or 11.

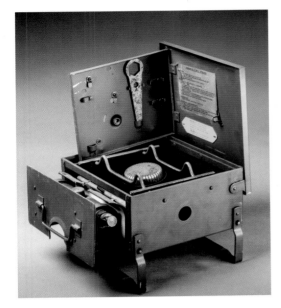

top condition at all times, hence the 'slave to the tank park' mentality mentioned above. Chieftain crewmen were confident in both their level of training and their deep and intimate understanding of the tank that they crewed, and there is absolutely no doubt that they regarded the tank with a huge amount of pride and affection.

The end of the line

The replacement for Chieftain was being considered under GSR 1008 as early as June 1961 – more than five years before it actually entered service. This may seem extraordinary, but actually represents prudent forward planning, because of the long timescales involved in getting a new MBT into service. Seventeen years later, in June 1978, the Defence Equipment Policy Committee finally decided that the Chieftain replacement should be:

■ Developed and produced in the UK;
■ Of conventional design; and
■ Mount a 120mm rifled gun.

This was intended to be the MBT80 but ended up as Challenger; a fuller version of the story of how Chieftain was eventually replaced is told in the Haynes Manual *Challenger 1 Main Battle Tank*.

Once the Chieftains were no longer required, they were disposed of – Struck Off

ABOVE A 4th/7th Dragoon Guards (4/7DG) KAPE (Keep the Army in the Public Eye) tour in 1976. These tours were designed to aid recruiting and to allow the public to forge closer links with their local regiment. *(Courtesy Bob Griffin)*

ABOVE LEFT Just as the boresight was critical for shooting straight, this was as important in keeping the crew fed: the No 2 petrol cooker. *(TM 10067.001)*

Strength (SOS) in the military vernacular. There were a number of fates that awaited them, some sadder than others. The majority were sold to scrap merchants for melting down, destroyed by the military under the reduction of Conventional Forces in Europe scheme (Operation ABANET), or used as range targets, where they would be expected to last for many years due to the excellent armour that they were built with.[18] Others became training aids, some were used as 'gate guardian' plinth vehicles (the majority in military barracks but a couple in civilian locations), and not a few ended up either with private owners or in various museums; the Tank Museum, Bovington, not surprisingly having a superb selection, from prototypes and 'funnies' to a Mk 11. The last Chieftain MBT finally left British Army service nearly 30 years after the first tank had entered it: on 22 March 1996, the 24-year-old 00FD90

---

18 Chieftain never served on the British bases in Cyprus until it was retired, when five tanks were shipped there to be used as hard targets on ranges.

MY ANTIPODEAN AFFAIR

Maj J.D. Muir RAAC

After I had cut my teeth on Centurion in 1969 including a tour of Vietnam, I had been fortunate enough to have been a student on the British Long Armour Infantry Course (LAIC) at Bovington in 1974, where I had been introduced to Chieftain. My secondment to 3RTR in BAOR in 1983 as OC B Sqn was therefore not my first exposure to the beast. In-between times I had been converted to Leopard AS1 in 1976 and thought very highly of it. Leopard AS1 was the Australian version of Leopard 1 with a much upgraded computerised gunnery system. I came to Paderborn with both great excitement about the posting but with a feeling that Chieftain must be nearing the end of its life. Unfortunately, I had been the Regimental Technical Adjutant at the 1st Armoured Regiment (Australia) in 1975, when Centurion was on its last legs and I was therefore anticipating similar mechanical and lack of spare parts problems with Chieftain. To cut a long story short, I was wrong: I fell in love with my tank 00FD19. It was even fast; yes, you heard me right … but more of that later.

It was also reliable, breaking down only once in my two-and-a-quarter-year posting. I can only applaud the dedication and expertise of my crew, and also the quite excellent REME fitter troop who worked tirelessly to keep us all on the road. The tank had a 120mm gun as opposed to the 105mm of Leopard, a real buzz for me, and it was surrounded by a squadron of soldiers with whom I would be happy to go to war. As an old gunnery officer, I recall discussing techniques with the gunnery instructors in 3RTR, and with my then loader/operator Cpl Dick Taylor, who although quite excellent as a radio operator was hell-bent on becoming a gunnery instructor himself. I explained to him that I thought that the techniques we were using for APDS were a little cumbersome and that they could be shortened by understanding the trajectory of the APDS round. Given a first-round miss you would either see the ground-strike in front of the target, or not see a strike, which indicated a high round. At 2,000m, a simple top edge or bottom edge of target correction would see the second round on target. Of course, there was not unanimous agreement, but I recall LCpl Bruce Hockings, my faithful (and obedient) gunner, following my instructions on the ranges at Hohne and BATUS with great success.

The amusing – and at times less amusing – incidents that occurred were often a result of my new environment. Having been used, in Australia, to dedicated training areas in the outback, training in the German countryside and on public roads was something I needed to master. In the days before mobiles I thought it a nice touch that, as the Sqn Commander, I was issued with my own telephone, to make what I assumed would be trunk calls whilst parked in one of the many forests.

I was also amused by what seemed to be a British class-related sleeping arrangement where I remained awake in the turret whilst my energetic crew were outside.

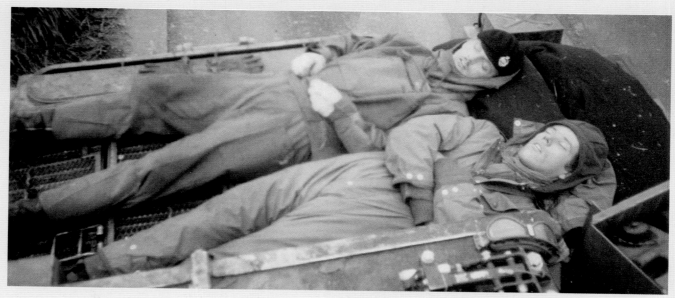

I was not always so amused while learning to cope with the local countryside and what appeared to be left-over Second World War tank ditches: as a student of tank technology I am sure the designers of Chieftain got the ground clearance wrong.

The best I could manage of a poor situation, which everyone seemed determined to photograph, was a meagre attempt at 'hull down'.

I was then, and am now, eternally grateful for the thoughtful, dedicated and loyal nature of my 2IC, Capt Stephen Harrison. It was Stephen who again highlighted my concern about the design of Chieftain when he found himself bogged on Exercise MEDICINE MAN 5 in BATUS.

I could only watch, somewhat embarrassed for him – and be thankful that it was not me. On a more serious note, and in comparison, I found Centurion to be the right tank for its time in South Vietnam, the Leopard 1AS the right tank for Australia's then likely theatre of combat, and the Chieftain the tank in which I would have felt most comfortable had we deployed for the real thing in Germany.

Oh, I almost forgot, I said it was fast. Let me explain. I was probably quite well known within 3RTR for being somewhat forthright with my opinions, and on more than one occasion I boasted that I believed that I had the fastest tank in the regiment. This was put to the test by the CO, John Woodward, and his 2IC, Patrick Dealtry, at the end of a training exercise on SLTA. Patrick announced over the radio that the OC's tanks of B and C Sqns would engage in a race. The race was approximately 500m cross-country followed by a U-turn and then back the same distance to the finishing line. Patrick then announced what I am sure he thought would be the end of my bragging, by stating that the tanks had to be driven by the respective Sqn Commanders. Patrick had obviously forgotten about my time at Bovington. The race was run, the race was won, and dear old 00FD19 was never challenged again.

BELOW Maj John Muir was an experienced tank commander, having served on Centurion in Vietnam, and Leopard in Australia. He proved to be a fantastic squadron leader who was loved by his crews and really understood what Chieftain was all about, commanding B Sqn 3RTR in BAOR and in BATUS.

ABOVE An immaculately presented Mk 11 00FD90 belonging to 1RTR, photographed as it was about to leave the unit on 22 March 1996, thereby ending nearly three decades of Chieftain MBT in British Army service. Despite being in such good condition (and older than the soldier who drove her), she ended up as a range target on the Castlemartin ranges in Wales.

BELOW Operation ABANET: 00FC04 being prepared for destruction by explosive, under the terms of the Conventional Forces Europe (CFE) agreement.

belonging to the CO of 1RTR was struck off unit strength and sent to the depot at Ludgershall, awaiting disposal. It was very fitting that 1RTR should be entrusted to see Chieftain out of service, as it was crews from that regiment, alongside 5RTR, who had carried out the very first troop trials in December 1962.

J.A.'S FOLLY – OR THE LONGEST JOCKEY

By Tpr A.D. Fisher 3RTR

B Sqn 3RTR deployed on Exercise MEDICINE MAN 1 at BATUS Canada in April 1977. This would be my first of many stints out on the prairies of Alberta. Just before we flew out to Canada fate took its course and our poor troop leader, one Lt Ashley-Birtwhistle, on exchange from the 14/20H, was injured in a car crash. This, of course, caused a manning problem, but one which was quickly resolved by moving the troop sergeant up to become the troop leader, the troop corporal therefore became the troop sergeant, and the troop leader's normal radio operator/loader, L/Cpl John Alsop (J.A.), became the troop corporal. He inherited the remnants of the troop leader's crew, with me as the loader/operator rather than my usual job of driver, Tpr Smiler Neale stayed as gunner, and I was replaced in the cab by a brand new driver in the shape of Bob (Titch) Rice, who had yet to be on an exercise, let alone BATUS. Titch was so small that he needed to have a sleeping bag behind his back in order to push him far enough forward to reach the pedals. I should point out at this stage that J.A. was not a qualified tank commander and was therefore under quite a bit of pressure as BATUS was not the ideal place to start one's career as a commander, particularly with such an inexperienced crew.

J.A. would be the first to admit that he was slow to find his feet and during the first couple of days out on the vast expanse of prairie we found ourselves 'geographically embarrassed' (lost) on several occasions. The live firing exercises steadily grew in their complexity until we arrived at the withdrawal exercise. The night before the exercise Sgt Skip Hilton, the acting troop leader, called J.A. over and said to him 'Don't worry, we won't leave you behind tomorrow' – much to J.A'.s relief. The next morning as the sun rose in the sky we were informed by our Safety Staff that we could go to 'Action' and begin live firing. Targets started to appear, which we fired at and we seemed to be holding our own – usually a fair bet against a cardboard enemy. They then started to appear more frequently and got closer, causing the Sqn OC to order the troop to withdraw in line with the nature of this particular exercise. J.A. told Titch to reverse and we came back off the ridge into a small coulee or valley, conducting a manoeuvre called jockeying. This involved reversing into dead ground, and then, whilst out of sight of the enemy, swinging the hull around 180° so that the driver could withdraw at top speed whilst the gun was over the back decks, still pointing at the advancing enemy and able to fire if necessary.

We'd been moving for a couple of minutes or so and the panic was rising in J.A.'s voice as he was looking over his shoulder, peering through his periscopes; for safety reasons we had to be fully closed down under armour. He shouted that the other two tanks in the troop were pulling ahead, and then at Titch asking him if he was in top gear with his foot flat down, which he said he was. Meanwhile, Smiler and I were enduring a real roller-coaster ride inside the turret as Titch seemed to have the uncanny knack of finding every big bump on the prairie – and I'd never heard an L60 revved so hard. I remember thinking to myself that something wasn't quite right … at the peak of our torture in the gloom of the turret I looked down at the turret floor and then the penny dropped. What I should have been able to see was the back of the driver's seat and Titch's head, but all I could see were the hull charge bins. With a grin I just sat back and watched J.A. continuing to rage about the other two tanks leaving us far behind. After a minute J.A. realised that I was laughing and shouted at me 'What the hell are you finding so funny?' I just pointed at the charge bins: his shoulders sagged and then he smiled which in turn changed to him laughing like a drain. He guided Titch around while using the gun kit to keep the gun pointing down range, so that the hull was – finally – pointing in the right direction and we headed off towards the rest of the troop, who were waiting on the next ridge line. The ride was understandably both much faster and smoother.

Of course we all blamed Titch but he didn't know any better. When J.A. had asked him was he in top gear, he was – as far as he was concerned. He was in high reverse and driving as fast as he could, about six miles an hour tops, without being able to see the ground that he was reversing over and giving us such an excruciating ride. At the end of the jockey off the ridge J.A. had forgotten to guide Titch around so that he was pointing in the right direction, away from the enemy … so we had motored for about ten minutes in high reverse, wondering why we couldn't keep up with the other two tanks who were going flat out in sixth gear. In hindsight, in the high-pressure environment of BATUS it was the sort of mistake that even a more experienced (and qualified) commander might make, and when I came to command there myself a few short years later, I ensured that I did not repeat the error ... but to this day I wonder what the Safety Staff who was supervising us, sat in his Redtop Ferret, must have thought of our long-distance jockey.

BELOW What the jockey *should* have looked like: with the gun pointing in the general direction of the enemy, the commander has guided his driver around so that they can withdraw at top speed. The red markings here show that this tank is playing the enemy, and in action (and BATUS) the crew would be closed down. *(Courtesy Carl Schulze)*

	MBT Mk 1	MBT Mk 2	MBT Mk 3	MBT Mk 5
Eqpt Code	0300-2010	0300-2020	0300-2030	0300-2050
Weight unladen lb	116,720	115,600	119,280	120,813
Bridge class laden	56			60
Height turret top	8' 3"			
Height overall	9' 5"			9' 6"
Length gun rear	32' 0"			
Length gun front	35' 5"	35' 5"		35' 8"
Width overall	12' 0"			
Width over tracks	10' 11"			
Ground clearance	20"			
L60	Mk 4A 585bhp	Mk 4A 650bhp	Mk 5A 650bhp	Mk 7A 720bhp
H30	Mk 7A		Mk 10A	
TN12	Mk 3			
Max speed	25.3mph			27mph
Max speed reverse	6mph			9mph
Comd's day sight	No 36	No 37 Mk 1	No 37 Mk 2 or 3	No 37 Mk 3 or 4
PRI	No 6	No 7		No 12 or 13
Comd's night sight	Nil	L1A1 (II)		L1A1
Comd's periscopes	1 × No 26 1 × No 27 7 × No 31	9 × No 40 Mk 1		9 × 40 Mk 2
Gnr's day sight	No 32	No 38		No 59 or TLS No 1
Gnr's telescope	No 26			No 70
Gnr's night sight	No 33 (IR)	L1A1 (II)		
Dvr's day sight	No 36			
Dvr's night sight	Nil	L2A1		L4A1
GCE	No 7 Mk 4			No 7 Mk 5

Source: technical handbooks.

The export saga

Centurion had proved an extremely attractive tank for export sales: of the nearly 4,500 built, more than half went to over a dozen export customers. This brought in an estimated £200 million and around three times that in ammunition and spares. This was seen to be good value for a tank whose design and development had cost the UK no more than £5 million. In July 1966, a Treasury report estimated that, up to that point, Chieftain had cost £15.5 million to develop, which understandably was used as the main reason to seek similarly large export sales. By 1968 it was over £20 million, one-third of which was on post-production modifications and development. The Treasury was keeping a

close watch on the rising costs and therefore pushed the MoD to support export drives, and during the early 1960s hopes were high that Chieftain would be sold to a number of European countries. During its development, one eye was always kept on increasing the export potential. For example, after prototype W5 had completed over 6,000 miles in only two years between February 1962 and February 1964, a progress meeting suggested removing the engine and stripping it down for examination; if all was 'as expected', the results could be used as 'worthwhile sales propaganda'. Britain let it be known that any country wishing to trial Chieftain could loan one or more tanks for six to nine months in order to try them out, which Israel in particular made full use of (more of which presently).

There is no doubt that the continual requests for demonstrations to the international military community, and the Germans in particular, interfered with the attempts to bring the tank into service: in May 1963, Maj Gen Hutton, Director General Fighting Vehicles (DGFV), asked for 'the initiation of action to stop this waste of time and effort'. He can only have had limited success, as on 17/18 July 1963 the UK staged a major demonstration of Chieftain's capabilities, focusing on firepower, at the Kirkcudbright ranges. Four Chieftains were used, and a large number of friendly nations were invited, including all NATO and Commonwealth countries, plus Sweden and Switzerland. On 1 August 1967 another large demonstration of Chieftain – much improved by this time but by no means perfect – took place at Bovington to defence officials from no less than 36 nations … it cannot be said that they weren't trying.

Germany

At the same time that the Chieftain prototypes were being produced and its capabilities were able to be demonstrated, a rival entered the market, in the form of the German Standard Panzer, later named Leopard. In some ways a two-horse race developed for many export markets; the choice was between a simple, fast, but only moderately armoured and armed tank (Leopard), and a complex, somewhat unreliable but exceptionally heavily armed and armoured tank (Chieftain).

At the start of the 1960s the two nations had agreed to buy two of the other nation's tanks in order to assess them fully. At one point the Treasury directly stepped into the export arena and suggested that co-operation could take the form of Britain supplying the heavy (Chieftain) tanks for both nations, and Germany the mediums (Leopard); needless to say, neither country wanted to go down the route of a two-tank fleet. Notwithstanding this, the 'Gamma' demonstration for German officials took place at Kirkcudbright in November 1962, designed to demonstrate the outstanding performance of the 120mm – because the tank was struggling with automotive issues, it made sense to concentrate on the two best aspects of the tank, firepower and survivability. (The code

name of the demonstration derived from the letter G, which meant Germany.)

German tank personnel had completed training in the UK by October 1965. Two of the prototypes (re-registered for military sales as 05MS98 and 99) were prepared, and for some reason were fitted with the underpowered early Mk 3A L60 engines, Mk 7A GUEs and the No 11 cupola; it is amazing that two of the newly built Mk 1s were not substituted instead. They arrived in the German proving establishment in Meppen in January 1966, and were officially handed over on 21 February, starting their gunnery trials the following day. The subsequent British observer's report on the trials makes it clear that the Germans were lukewarm about the whole process, and did not bother to service the tanks or set them up correctly before firing. Whether this was due to the (reported) poor quality of their crews, to the complexity of the tanks or because of other more nefarious reasons is not clear, but what is evident is that the trials were doomed from the outset. Both German-owned tanks eventually ended up in museums in the USA.

Belgium and the Netherlands

Britain saw these two countries as linked, believing that if they could make a sale to one, their neighbour might follow. It was believed that the Belgians would be interested in Chieftain because they required about 300 new tanks to replace their old American types, and a presentation was delivered in Brussels in December 1964. However, for fairly obvious reasons, they turned out to be more interested in the French AMX30 or the German Leopard; they were not only far simpler for conscripts to operate but also much cheaper than Chieftain, with the French tank estimated at £100K each and Leopard costing £110K, against Chieftain's £130K. The *Daily Mail* of 9 September 1965 reported that the UK was considering offering a £10K discount per tank to sweeten the deal, as well as allowing the Belgians to manufacture the engines and transmissions as offset, but the tank was thought to be too complicated and underpowered, as well as suffering from by-then notorious unreliability. (In fact the *Mail* was wildly wrong: the actual price being offered was £90K.)

At around the same time, the Dutch were anticipated to be in the market to buy up to 550 new tanks around 1970. Partly to offset the mounting criticism of Chieftain, particularly in what was perceived to be unfair comparisons with Leopard, Exercise VERITAS was carried out in Long Valley on Friday, 10 June 1966, with visitors including the Dutch Deputy Chief of the General Staff (DCGS) and the Inspector of Cavalry. The exercise featured a range of mobility tests in which Chieftains, the British-owned Leopards and the then-current Dutch tank, Centurion Mk 5, were directly compared. Chieftain proved it could climb steep slopes that Leopard (and Centurion) could not, and despite the accusations of being underpowered, was only slightly slower than Leopard cross-country, as the table demonstrates:

EXERCISE VERITAS ACCELERATION TEST

	0–100M	0–200M	0–300M	0–400M	0–500M
Centurion 5	15s	25.6s	36s	46.5	56.2
Leopard	14.5s	22.2s	29.8s	36.9s	42.4s
Chieftain	15s	25s	33.5s	42.2s	49.8s

Source: Tank Museum records.

BELOW Exercise VERITAS 1966: the Dutch Inspector of Cavalry, Col Van Balluseck, was determined to select Leopard for his country and looks inscrutable (or should that be uninterested?) as he is shown how to drive Chieftain.

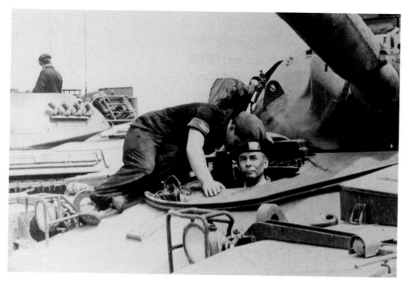

Despite Leopard having 20.6bhp per ton, against Chieftain's 650bhp engine giving only 12.9bhp per ton, Leopard won, but not as convincingly as many expected; had a 750bhp engine been available for Chieftain, the results would have been much closer. Insufficient emphasis was placed on the key figures in the first column, the ability to accelerate away from a standing start, which adds to battlefield survivability: in this respect, Leopard had no meaningful advantage. This test was reinforced by others which showed that Chieftain was much more able to make use of its power due to the excellent Horstmann suspension and semi-automatic gearbox. Although Leopard was impressive over flat fields and the like, Chieftain was faster over more complex and testing terrain. One commentator – British and therefore admittedly biased – stated that 'It is felt that Leopard has paid dearly in firepower and protection for an increase in mobility which will, more often than not, be unusable on the battlefield.' Britain was convinced that it had learned the lessons of the Second World War by fielding a tank which could both take a hit and deal out impressive punishment, and which was suited to the type of warfare expected in Europe. It was felt that Germany, on the other hand, had moved too far away from the heavy tanks it had been obsessed with during the war and was determined to field a medium tank rather than a true MBT. One report of September 1965 quoted a German officer as saying that Leopard was based upon what they would have wanted in a tank in Russia in 1943, and was not designed for defensive combat in western Europe.

Exercise CRACKLE demonstrated Chieftain in the Netherlands from January to May 1968, leading to 'much criticism of the 650bhp engine'. The Dutch crews also carried out live firing using the German ranges at Meppen, just over the border – no doubt the German experts there took careful note of the results. One of the engines failed at 1,400 miles,[19] and the Dutch were adamant that they would only be interested in Chieftain if it had a reliable 750bhp engine. But by this stage many British officials realised that there was little chance of a sale

---

19 The equivalent of over two years' usage in BAOR.

even if the tank possessed a 750bhp engine that was 100% reliable, as it was known that the head of the Dutch armoured corps had his heart set on Leopard. By the end of 1968 there was no realistic chance of making a sale, and the *Daily Mail* reported the collapse of negotiations and the purchase of 415 Leopards for £56 million on 25 October 1968. (The final part of the Dutch saga relates to them showing a sudden but short-lived interest in Shir 2 with Chobham armour around 1977.)

Israel

During 1966 the Israelis were concerned that neighbouring Arab nations were being equipped with the new T62, and were talking in terms of buying 300 Chieftains, with 100 supplied direct from the UK and the remainder to be built by Israeli Military Industries under licence locally. It was thought that such a sale would bring in around £10 million, excluding the spares requirement and ammunition. Chieftain's thick armour, excellent firepower, overall survivability and 10° of MA depression all suited the Israeli concept of a defensive tank that protected the crew to the maximum extent. However, they also wanted a tank that had dependable mobility for when it was needed, and as their army was comprised mainly of conscripts, it had to be simple and easy to maintain too. Britain was prepared to loan two tanks for up to four years to secure the sale. For secrecy the overall project was referred to as Exercise ADULATE.

No 1RTR were responsible for carrying out the first Chieftain hot/dusty trials in Aden from June until September 1966, called Exercise HOTSHOT 1, in the course of which their two brand new tanks (02EB44 and 47) fired 286 MA rounds.[20] Although these trials became linked to the Israeli interest, they were probably scheduled anyway. Exercise HOTSHOT 2 was a purely export-driven affair, and took place at Nahal-Tsinim, near Sde-Boker in Israel in 1967. The two tanks loaned free of charge to the IDF were there during the Six-Day War in June.[21] Although there has been much speculation that the Israelis used these tanks in combat, in truth this is extremely unlikely, partly as they were nowhere near the front lines and particularly as a party of British soldiers accompanied the tanks. Following this, in Exercise RISSOLE 1, two upgraded tanks were then sent to Israel in December 1967 accompanied by an officer and two REME experts. During the trials that followed in the Sinai Desert, both MEs failed in February 1968 at around the 1,500-mile mark, mainly due to sand ingress. For the subsequent Exercise RISSOLE 2, another two new tanks left the UK on 14 May 1968, having been modified following the many Israeli criticisms of the tank after the first exercise, the main one of which was pretty straightforward to state but much more difficult to do – make the tank reliable in desert conditions.

ABOVE A Chieftain being used to test dust ingress; note the collection tubes and the instrumentation on the turret roof. As it has a No 11 cupola and the early pattern rear bins, it is probably a Mk 1. *(Courtesy Brian Clark)*

20 This must have been a somewhat secret operation as the details were not entered on the vehicle record cards.

21 The IDF had to pay for transportation, spares and ammunition.

Sufficient improvements must have been made, however, as the Israelis made a firm offer to buy 250 Chieftains (as well as 250 more Centurions) on 17 October 1968, which was agreed in principle on 13 November, with deliveries to begin one year later. At least five Israeli soldiers 'experienced on Centurion' attended training courses in the UK. Both governments wanted to keep the negotiations secret until completed, but somehow the cat escaped the bag and the Kuwaitis lodged objections in March 1969. However, before any tanks were built or supplied, the UK government had a change of heart and used the sale as a bargaining tool, in order to try and bring about peace in the Middle East. On 1 May 1969, the Foreign Secretary, Michael Stewart, told the Israeli Ambassador that 'the present is not an appropriate time to conclude an understanding … we will review the decision in autumn 1969'. Concurrently, preparations were being made to supply the first batch of tanks should the deal be ratified;

under Exercise WAYSIDE, 15 Mk 3/2 tanks were to sail for Israel in December 1969, with another three in kit form the following March. Exercise BLENHEIM was also being conducted in Israel from June to August 1969 whilst the British position was hardening, to test 'recent engine developments and gunnery equipment, including a laser rangefinder, in desert conditions'. Involved were two brand new Mk 2 tanks, 05EB32 and 33, fitted with the latest Mk 5A 650bhp engines.

The final decision not to supply Chieftains to Israel was taken in late 1969, and the Israeli military (mainly in the person of General Tal) was incensed, as much by their perception that they had been deceived as by the actual decision itself, clearly not realising that diplomacy often involves lying, even if the lies are delivered by politicians with ritual politeness and a smile. As a direct result, the Israelis set out to design their own tank, which resulted in the Merkava. The final two trial Chieftains returned from Israel on 23 March 1970.

BELOW General Tal, photographed next to one of the trial Chieftains in Israel; note the black and white markings along the bazooka plates, and that the tank appears to have an Israeli registration. *(TM 6010E2)*

Nonetheless, two Chieftains were either built or more probably converted (from Mk 3)[22] to the Mk 4 automotive standard in 1970 specifically to Israeli requirements, the most significant of which was the redesign of the rear hull to allow 100 gallons more fuel to be carried. A 750bhp engine was used for the first time, giving a higher power-to-weight ratio; this had a larger low-loss air cleaner mounted to it, in order to reduce the dust ingress into the L60. The addition of extra weight to the rear necessitated moving the centre and rear Horstmann units rearwards – with roadwheel 4 nearly touching number 5 – and an additional top roller unit was mounted above the gap between 2 and 3.

Other very specific changes were requested by the Israelis to be fitted to the Mk 4s; for example, because of the ranges they expected to fight at, the Israeli version of the No 37 commander's sight was required to have a magnification of ×15. They wanted both an LRF and an extended range RG, which tells us that the Israelis understood that the laser might not be totally reliable and that having a back-up in the form of the .50 Browning would be sensible. When it became available they also wanted both computerised fire control and passive night vision to be fitted. The British, despite not being able to make the considerable amount of cash expected from the export, did gain a lot of benefit in the long run, as the Israeli comments and the results of the various trials were fed into the other developmental work being undertaken, which helped to make the tank automotively more reliable; the two Mk 4 tanks were used for extensive dust testing at Yuma Proving Ground in 1971.

As an interesting final aside, one of the capacious files in the National Archives dealing with this topic tells the following tale: an enterprising British officer working in Defence Security had discovered that the Israelis had captured a number of Soviet T55 tanks, and the British were extremely keen to examine some. In February 1970 he suggested that, when the next batch of Centurions were sent to Israel, Britain should 'slip a further five Centurions on to the tail of this order, at no cost to the Israelis,

22 This assumption is based on the date, as well as the configuration – the Mk 4s had the new pairs of smaller headlights, but the L11A2 gun.

ABOVE One of the two Mk 4s built for Israel, showing the modified rear hull with additional fuel capacity; note the larger rear stowage bins and twin turret baskets used to compensate for the loss of the long tool bins along each side.
(Courtesy Chris Trigg)

in exchange for five T55s'. The reaction to this was not recorded.

Libya

Another nation that definitely wanted Chieftain and approached Britain requesting them was Libya, with an order code-named Exercise DELICATE placed for 188 Mk 3/1 tanks in early 1969, comprising 125 gun tanks, 37 command variants, 9 dozers, 14 Armoured Recovery Vehicles (ARVs) and 3 Armoured Vehicle Launched Bridges (AVLBs). They were to cost £25.5 million and were meant to be delivered over 36 months from November 1970. Complications were caused by the overthrow of King Idris in September 1969 and the installation of a new revolutionary government. The new leader, Colonel Qaddafi (who had seen Chieftain when he attended a course at Bovington), still wanted the tanks, but the British government were not convinced by his promise not to use them outside the country nor to pass them on, and saw the sale as a bargaining tool to improve the chances of a Middle East peace settlement. Libya was still pressing for the order to be completed in March 1972, in part because an advance of £9.5 million had been paid in May 1969, but Britain was loathe to supply the tanks and gave them the same answer that had been given to the Israelis, that it would be reconsidered only when the political situation was improved. None were supplied.

ABOVE A newly
made Chieftain
ready for shipping
to Iran, complete

ABOVE A newly
made Chieftain
ready for shipping
to Iran, complete
with its military sales
registration. This has
a combination of both
the RG and TLS with
MRS, which would be
rare in British service.

Iran

Strange as it may seem today, but in the late
1960s relations between Israel and Iran were
better than cordial, and the Israeli General Tal,
heavily involved in trying to secure hundreds of
Chieftains for his own nation, recommended
that the Iranian armoured corps purchase the
tank; he even assisted them in defining their
own specification, which included the familiar
demand that the engine must produce 750bhp.
As a result, 707 Chieftains were ordered by
Iran in January 1971 and had been delivered
by 1978, along with 14 AVLBs and 41 ARVs.[23]
ROFL built 567 of the MBTs, the remaining 140
were built by Vickers at Elswick. The vehicles
were delivered in a special camouflage paint
known as 'Semi-Gloss Persian Drab', later
camouflaged with broad irregular stripes of
brown. The Imperial Iranian Ground Forces
often invited British companies to test and
demonstrate new tank systems to them in Iran.
One such demonstration concerned proposed
air conditioning kits for both Chieftain and
Scorpion, and took place at Ahwaz in southern
Iran, the home of the 92nd Armoured Division,
in August and September 1975. Two Iranian

Chieftains were supplied for the demonstration,
43MS82 and 91 (other known registrations
used were 45MS71 and 48MS40, which gives
us a range that includes over 450 of the tanks).
Of the initial 707 Chieftains, 73 were Mk 3/3Ps,
and 634 were Mk 5/1Ps.[24] The first 215 tanks
supplied to Iran had the L11A3 gun; all the
remainder mounted the L11A5 gun.

Then another order was placed for Mk 5/3P,
also known as FV 4030/1. Despite fierce
competition from the Germans and the USA, and
notwithstanding Iranian concerns over poor L60
reliability in the existing fleet, Iran asked Britain
to develop an updated model of the Chieftain,
known in official circles as the Fighting Vehicle
Project 4030 Phase 1 or FV4030/1 and often
referred to as the Improved Chieftain.[25] This was
because the Iranians wanted a tank with the
best combination of 'endurance, robustness,
heavy armour and first-class armament' and only
Chieftain could meet the requirement, despite
its known defects. A total of 193 of these were
ordered (to bring the overall total of MBTs up to
a round 900), and 185 had been delivered by
1979. The main reason for such a small interim

---

23 A total of 73 ARVs were ordered, but it appears that only 41 were
delivered. Up to 175 Armoured Repair and Recovery Vehicles (ARRVs)
were on order but none were delivered.

24 P stood for Persia.

25 By 1975 Iran was using significant quantities of the L60 Mk 8 engine,
which compared very favourably with the US M60 tanks also operated
by them.

order was the need to keep the British production line at Leeds gainfully employed until a more automotively capable tank could be ordered; over 90% of the capacity at ROFL was being employed on the Iranian vehicles and, without an order to keep it going, the factory might have closed.[26] The vehicles were built between August 1976 and late 1977/early 1978, and featured TLS and MRS, a fully automatic controller for the gearbox, a 50-gallon fuel capacity increase, thickened underbelly mine armour and shock absorbers fitted to the rear suspension units.

In 1974 another interim order for 100 tanks was placed, to be known as Shir 1 (FV4030/2), but which was still, in essence, Chieftain, but with a new 1,200bhp CV12 engine and TN37 gearbox. Originally it was intended to replace the L60 with an 800bhp version of the constant velocity (CV) engine, in order to simplify the project as this would not have required major alterations to the shape of the hull, but this was then rejected in favour of the larger engine and new gearbox.[27] The first three Shir 1 prototypes were ready by January 1979, with deliveries due to commence in July 1979 at a unit price of £700K. These tanks were not delivered, as the Iranians repudiated the contract in March 1979, but Leeds had a large stockpile of materials and parts, and some tanks were partially assembled. (The Shah had also come close to ordering 175 ARVs fitted with the CV12 engine, but pulled out at the last minute.) Before the contract was repudiated, plans were in place to retrofit TLS and MRS to the Mk 3/3P and 5/1P tanks, starting in June 1978, to be followed by an IFCS retrofit planned for the whole fleet (including Shir 1) starting in 1983.

British support to the Iranian Armour Centre at Shiraz – home of the grape – was extensive: in 1971 the first five REME artificers were posted there to support the introduction of Chieftain. In January 1979, amidst the turmoil of the revolution, it was decided to evacuate the British personnel, but three retired REME

officers supporting the project were captured at gunpoint, blindfolded and held in a prison where they genuinely expected to be executed. After being detained for what was described with remarkable understatement as 'a few harrowing days', they were released.

The Iranian Chieftains were used in the fighting with Iraq in the extended war from 1980 to 1988, where the L60 engine again caused problems, particularly with overheating, but this time probably due more to a lack of spare parts and technical know-how. A damage assessment report made by a British civilian team during the Iran–Iraq War allowed them to see how Chieftain – particularly the armour – was standing up to combat with modern threats, and led to other improvements being made to the British fleet, including additional armour in the form of Stillbrew. However, the report indicated that, in general, the survivability measures built into Chieftain had worked well when the tank was hit, making it popular with the Iranian crews because it not only resisted strikes but also allowed them time to get out if it was penetrated. After-action reports from Iranian crewmen revealed how poorly trained the crews were after the British support staff had been withdrawn, with one tank commander relating how he was sent to the front-line having only ever fired the MA on the simulator, and not once for real on a range. In 2006, Jane's estimated that Iran still had around 200 of the fleet in service or storage, but at the time of writing it is thought that only around 100–150 of the original Chieftains are still on strength, and their condition can only be guessed at, although it is believed that efforts were made to re-engine and update some into a version known as Mobarez (Duellist), although exact details are unclear.

Jordan

In 1979 Jordan owned a fleet of 278 Centurions (amongst other types), and was investigating the option of refurbishing them to bring them to something approaching modern standards. When the UK was looking for potential buyers for the partially built ex-Iranian Shir 1 tanks, Jordan immediately opened negotiations, and despite other nations – including Syria – showing interest in the Shir 1, it was Jordan who secured them and renamed them Khalid, opting

---

26 Eight of the Mk 5/3Ps were in the UK for MVEE trials when the contract was cancelled; their fate is unknown but they may have been used in the Khalid and Challenger development programmes.

27 This might have provided a realistic export version of Chieftain, giving it a reasonable power-to-weight ratio and reliability with no major structural alterations needed for those already-operating fleets equipped with the L60. Interestingly, by November 1975, the Iranians were operating 280 Chieftains fitted with the Mk 8 L60 engine, which compared favourably with the M60s they were also using.

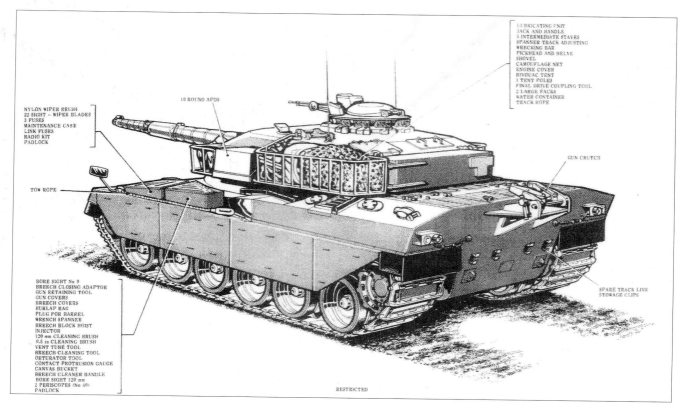

NYLON WIPER BRUSH
22 SIGHT – WIPER BLADES
3 FUSES
MAINTENANCE CASE
LINK FUSES
RADIO KIT
PADLOCK

10 ROUND APDS

LUBRICATING UNIT
JACK AND HANDLE
5 INTERMEDIATE STAVES
SPANNER TRACK ADJUSTING
WRECKING BAR
PICKHEAD AND HELVE
SHOVEL
CAMOUFLAGE NET
ENGINE COVER
BIVOUAC TENT
3 TENT POLES
FINAL DRIVE COUPLING TOOL
2 LARGE PACKS
WATER CONTAINER
TRACK ROPE

GUN CRUTCH

TOW ROPE

SPARE TRACK LINK
STOWAGE CLIPS

BORE SIGHT No 9
BREECH CLOSING ADAPTOR
GUN RETAINING TOOL
GUN COVERS
BREECH COVERS
BURLAP BAG
PLUG FOR BARREL
WRENCH SPANNER
BREECH BLOCK HOIST
INJECTOR
120 mm CLEANING BRUSH
0.5 in CLEANING BRUSH
VENT TUBE TOOL
BREECH CLEANING TOOL
OBTURATOR TOOL
CONTACT PROTRUSION GAUGE
CANVAS BUCKET
BREECH CLEANER HANDLE
BORE SIGHT 120 mm
2 PERISCOPES (No 40)
PADLOCK

RESTRICTED

ABOVE One of the stowage diagrams produced for Khalid, which clearly shows the radically altered rear hull shape.

to buy the new tanks rather than upgrade the Centurions.[28] There were very few differences between the Shir 1 as designed for Iran and the Khalid as bought by Jordan; the major modifications were that Khalid had twin electric starters, different gunner's laser and driver's night sights, and a modified rear suspension unit with an additional shock absorber.

At one point in the negotiations there was a real possibility that Jordan might, in time, be persuaded to buy up to 600 of the new tanks, enough to equip two armoured divisions. Another figure mentioned was 278, which was the size of the existing Jordanian Centurion fleet which might be refurbished as an alternative to buying new tanks, but when the contract was signed on 28 November 1979 it was for 274 MBTs, along with 21 Chieftain ARRVs and 5 AVLBs.[29] The MBTs were built as 224 gun tanks, 37 Squadron Headquarters (SHQ) tanks and 13 Regimental Headquarters (RHQ) tanks, with differing radio

installations to suit. (When asked if they might be interested in Shir 2, the Jordanians stated that they did not need such a high level of protection, and certainly not the weight penalty that came with it.) The trials vehicle 05SP50 had a RG fitted, but the service tanks were delivered fitted with IFCS and MRS and no RG.

The story of the financial negotiations for Khalid is interesting. As the Iranians had already made a down payment of £44 million for the development of Shir 1 and Shir 2 tanks, the UK eventually used this to offset the price paid by Jordan and make the tanks cheaper and hence more attractive, but started negotiations by asking for £1 million each. It should be realised just how much the Jordanians wanted the Khalid: both the USA and USSR had indicated willingness to provide much cheaper tanks, with M60A3 being put on offer at half the price of Khalid in August 1979. But King Hussein knew which tank he favoured and, despite him using the threat of obtaining either American or Soviet tanks as a bargaining tool, Khalid was always the front-runner. It was just a case of establishing the right price, and it appears that the Jordanians eventually paid a unit price of £820K. Another contract was signed in April 1980 for the provision of ammunition, spares, tools, test

---

28 In January 1979 Jordan had expressed an interest in buying around 300 'Chieftains with CV12' – as this predates the Iranian repudiation of the contract, it indicates that the Jordanians wanted Khalid anyway, and, due to the Iranian actions, simply ended up getting them very much sooner.

29 Two days later the *Financial Times* incorrectly reported the figure as 275.

equipment and training aids. Israel, needless to say, was extremely unhappy about the deal but could not prevent it.

By November 1980, Jordan was encouraging its neighbour Iraq to adopt Khalid as their MBT, but as the Iran–Iraq War had just started, there was no way that the UK would sell Iraq weapons. It might be asked why Jordan was allowed to buy so many modern tanks whereas Israel, Syria and Egypt, all of whom pursued

ABOVE Shir 1, aka FV4030/2, was developed into the Khalid tank used by Jordan. The Pilkington Condor day/night sight was used in the cupola, and given the designation No 84 by the British. In service, the Jordanians mounted mesh stowage baskets along the bazooka plates, as the extra width was immaterial in the open desert.

BELOW The rear of Khalid, showing the angled rear hull needed to accommodate the CV12 powerpack. The additional power finally gave a Chieftain tank variant a respectable power-to-weight ratio, at 20.7bhp per ton. *(TM 6624E3)*

RIGHT A Mk 5/2K, destined for export to Kuwait. Note the lack of wading rail and Light Projector, plus the single headlamps and APDS projectile stowage bin in the turret basket. The colour used was 'Kuwait Drab' made by ICI.

Chieftain, were refused?[30] The records show that there was a great deal of concern over the sale, but eventually it was decided that Jordan was unlikely to act as an aggressor, and the special relationship enjoyed between Jordan and the UK tipped the balance; how much the knowledge that the USA – or worse still the USSR – would step in anyway if Britain refused to supply the tanks affected the decision is not clear, but it must have counted for something.

Kuwait

Kuwait ordered 165 Chieftain Mk 5/2Ks in 1971. The first batch of 12 tanks was delivered in October 1976, and the final 21 were delivered

---

30 In 1978 Egypt had asked to buy 200 Chieftains, and was stalled by being told it could have Vickers MBT, but not Chieftain 'for a few years as none were available'. They then tried to buy up to 1,000 Shir 2 for delivery starting in 1982 but again were refused. On 22 January 1979, Syria expressed an interest in buying 300–500 'Chieftains with Chobham', which was also refused.

BELOW The MTU-engined Chieftain, developed for Kuwait, but never ordered due to the Iraqi invasion in 1990. (Courtesy Mark Gilbert)

just a little behind schedule on 26 March 1980. Although the official REME history stated that, in 1990, the team there was supporting 235 Chieftains, there is no evidence that more were acquired, and indeed in 1989 the Iraqi military intelligence believed that the Kuwaitis were operating 165 Chieftains, as well as 6 M84s, 70 Vickers MBT Mk 1s and 40 (probably non-battleworthy) Centurions. Therefore, it seems likely that the REME were counting the Vickers tanks as part of their responsibility and that only the original 165 Chieftains were in service.

Their experience with Chieftains must have been generally positive, as in 1979 Kuwait asked for a quotation for the supply of 165 Shir 2s – presumably to replace the Chieftains one for one – for delivery beginning in 1983. It may be that they could not afford the asking price, or simply that they were a little slow and that Britain was already committed to developing Challenger from Shir 2, but whatever the reason they did not get Shir 2 and retained their Chieftains. By the end of the 1980s Kuwait was considering upgrading their Chieftain fleet by fitting a 1,000bhp MTU diesel engine and a new RENK transmission, but this was curtailed by the Iraqi invasion of 1990. A single prototype with the new engine and gearbox was developed by Vickers Defence Systems (VDS) and the German companies involved, and it is currently resident at the Yorkshire Air Museum.

The Kuwaiti Chieftains were organised into four regiments, two in 15 Mechanised Brigade in Shaiba, south of Kuwait City, and two in 35 Shaheed Armoured Brigade, seen as the premier formation. The 35 Brigade, including 36 Chieftains (of 7th and 8th Battalions with 26 and 10 tanks respectively) saw action defending Kuwait from the Iraqi invasion on 2 August 1990 in the area between Ali Al Salem airbase and Al Jahra, west of Kuwait City. Despite not having been able to boresight their tanks, and with scratch crews, the Chieftains effectively engaged Iraqi armour at around 1,500m, causing many casualties, including T72s, and delaying the advance of two Iraqi divisions. (No 15 Mechanised Brigade does not appear to have fought the invaders.) There were no reports of Chieftains being damaged or destroyed by enemy action. In the course of the invasion 36 members of the 66-strong

British Army support team were captured and taken to Baghdad as part of Saddam's highly illegal human shield; fortunately they were later released unharmed.

At the conclusion of the swift invasion, a total of 136 Kuwaiti Chieftains were reported to have been captured by Iraq, although at least some of the tanks (possibly as many as 29) managed to escape over the Saudi Arabian border. In October 1990 the author was serving at the RAC Gunnery School, Lulworth, and volunteered to join a small team whose role was to retrain the Kuwaiti crews in order for them to spearhead the advance to liberate their home country using these tanks; the project was cancelled in late December. Nearly 100 of them were reported as still being in use in the Iraqi Army in 1990, but shortly after this 83 of the tanks were returned to Kuwait, along with 67 Vickers MBT Mk 1s. In 2006, Jane's reported that 17 of the tanks still remained in Kuwaiti service/storage.

Iraq

Iraq never bought any Chieftains from Britain – apart from surplus 29 ARRVs acquired around 1980 from the unfulfilled Iranian order – but captured substantial quantities of MBTs from both Iran in the 1980s and then a reported 136 from Kuwait in 1990. Sixty-nine had been captured 'in more or less good condition' from the Iranians by November 1980, and Jane's estimated that, in total, Iraq captured between 200 and 300 Chieftains during the course of the Iran-Iraq War, 1980–88. With such a large number on their hands, Iraq approached the UK with a view to installing CV12 engines and bringing them up

to near-Khalid standard, but the UK would not entertain such a deal – although it went as far as working out the cost as an estimated £250K per tank. Jane's reported that, in late 1988, Iraq then gifted 90 of them to Jordan;[31] as Jordan was operating Khalid, it is presumed that they were used as a source of spare parts. In identifying the original source of the Iraqi Chieftains from photographs, it is useful to note that the Kuwaiti tanks did not have a wading rail fitted around the hull – most prominent in front of the driver's cab – whereas it appears that the Iranian versions did. The Kuwaiti Mk 5/2s also only used a single small headlight on each side of the hull front, and did not have the Light Projector fitted. The Iraqis appear to have mounted 12.7mm Degtyaryov-Shpagin Large-Calibre (DShK) MGs on at least some of the tanks that they pressed into service, and favoured a camouflage pattern of green and sand in broad stripes.

Oman

In early 1981, the Omani armoured forces consisted of only two squadrons of ageing Saladin armoured cars, plus six M60 tanks. Oman then decided that it wanted Chieftains, despite the USA suggesting it might be prepared to supply more M60 tanks for free in return for political concessions. The UK sales organisation IMS was hopeful that the Omanis might be persuaded to buy between 40 and 45 to form a full regiment, but this was not to be, and only half that number was purchased. The deal had to be hurried through as the tanks were needed in Muscat for

ABOVE Kuwaiti Chieftains (with no Light Projectors) photographed before the 1990 invasion, proudly flying national flags from their antennae.

---

31 Believed to be one Mk 3/3s (P) and the remainder Mk 5.

ABOVE A new Chieftain Mk 15, aka Qayd Al Ardh, ready for shipping to Oman. It bears the Arabic registration number 189. Note the ballistic protection plates in front of the gunner's sight. *(TM 2471B7)*

the National Day parade on 18 November 1981. The reason behind the haste was national pride and regional influence: the Sultan of Oman had personally decided that he wanted two squadrons of modern tanks, and that only Chieftains would do, but new tanks could not be available for an estimated two to two-and-a-half years.[32] Initially, 12 Mk 7/2Cs were leased in August 1981 from British WMR stocks; the term of the lease was for two years up to 31 July 1983, each tank costing £50K per year to rent. The tanks had TLS and MRS, No 6 NBC packs, L11A5 guns and L60 Mk 11A or 13A engines. Oman also wanted to buy two ARVs/ARRVs but at £2 million could not afford them; and so in October 1981 Jordan gave one Chieftain ARV (J) to Oman as a free gift to support the new Chieftain fleet.

The leased tanks were then purchased outright for £12 million in early 1984, and as part of the deal, another 15 brand new tanks were purchased and delivered in 1984/85, allowing the formation of two tank squadrons. These new tanks were referred to by the British as Mk 15 and by the Omanis as the Qayd Al Ardh. Based upon the proposed British Mk 13 standard (which never saw service) with the latest L60 Mk 14A engine, the most important modification was the fitting of the NANOQUEST L20 commander's sight incorporating a Type 520 LRF. Apparently the tanks cost £1.5 million each, but the Omanis later discovered that other Chieftains sold in the Middle East had cost nearer to £1 million, which understandably annoyed them somewhat. Later the Omanis investigated the possibility of replacing the L60 engines with the 800bhp CV8 version of the

Rolls-Royce Condor, but this turned out to be a very expensive option and was not pursued.

Other nations

Pakistan confirmed interest in buying up to 300 Chieftains in February 1967 but nothing came of it. Nearly a decade later, in 1976, the Indian Army let it be known that it was 'discreetly interested' in Chieftain: in reality they had got wind of the development of Shir 2 (FV4030/3) for the Iranians, and in June the British Defence Minister Roy Mason had publicly confirmed the existence of Chobham armour. As a result, keen interest in the tank was expressed by the Indian Deputy Chief of Army Staff. India indicated that they wanted to purchase between 200 and 300 at around £800K each, and possibly negotiate a licence to build some in India. The UK was loathe to do anything that might either interfere with the huge Iranian order or upset the balance of power in the subcontinent, and responded that, at the earliest, tanks would not be available until 1985, on completion of the Iranian contract. As an interim measure, the British offered to supply one trial Chieftain with an 800bhp CV8 engine and TN37 gearbox for £800K in late 1979; however, it would *not* have Chobham armour, which was what had almost certainly stimulated the most interest in Delhi. There was sufficient interest for the option to be costed, with an asking price of £870K each for a production run of not less than 120 tanks. Although it was reported in 1979 that the Indians were still displaying a surprising 'intensity of interest in the 4030/3 tank', they then pulled out, possibly because of the long timescales, but probably more likely because they realised that they were not going to obtain Chobham anytime soon, and so started the tortuous development of their own MBT, the Arjun.

During 1967 both Canada and Denmark expressed interest in Chieftains, the former considering buying around 50 as a heavy tank to bolster its Centurions, but sensibly decided not to mix the fleet, as there was next to no commonality between the tanks. And, finally, the Swiss showed something approaching serious interest, when two Chieftain Mk 3/3s were loaned to Switzerland for a year, including being tested on Exercise ROYAL CHIEF from August 1971 to March 1972; the tank type was not selected, probably in part because of its complexity.

---

32 For the same reason the Omanis decided not to purchase 'Improved Chieftain' with the 800bhp CV8 engine. There was also a suggestion by the UK that Jordan might be prepared to release some of their new Khalids to Oman instead, but this did not take place.

EXPORT VEHICLES BY MARK

Mk	Automotive	Turret and firepower	Remarks
3/1	As British Mk 3 with new air cleaner and hull/turret breathing.		Proposed Libyan variant, did not enter service.
3/2	As British Mk 3 fitted for an American radio system.		Initial Israeli variant, did not enter service.
3/3P	As British Mk 3/3 with minor modifications inc. Racal BCC radio harness and VRQ301 VHF radios; RG.		Iranian (Persia) variant. 73 made.
4	750bhp L60; increased fuel carriage (100 gallons); dust filtration equipment; low-loss air cleaner.	Extended range RG; LRF; passive night vision; extra ammunition stowage (computerised fire control to be fitted when available).	Proposed Israeli variant, did not enter service. Equipment code 0300-2040. One believed to have subsequently tested Hydrogas suspension.
5/1P	Additional 36 gallons' fuel; L60 Mk 8A; H30 Mk 10A.	As British Mk 5 with: radio modifications; GCE No 7 Mk 5; No 15 Mk 3 cupola; 42 charge bin containers; 10 projectile APDS stowage in turret basket; RG.	Iranian (Persia) variant. 634 made.
5/2K	Wading rails not fitted; single headlamps; relocated tow rope.	No Light Projector; modified stowage turret left side inc. APDS bin in basket; RG; MRS.	Kuwaiti variant. Sometimes referred to as 5/5K.
5/3P	As Mk 5/1P plus automatic gear controller, additional underbelly armour; improved suspension; additional 50 gallons' fuel.	TLS and MRS.	Iranian (Persia) variant. Aka FV 4030/1. 193 made, 185 delivered.
15	Modifications based on proposed Mk 13 MBT; new L20 Comd's sight with Ferranti 520 LRF; no wading rail; no RG; fitted with Light Projector, IFCS and MRS.		Omani variant, known as Qayd Al Ardh
Khalid	CV12 1,200bhp engine; TN37 gearbox; single headlamps.	No 84 Commander's sight; No 25 PRI; meteorological sensor; IFCS; Racal VRQ301C and PRM4031 radios in Clansman harness.	Jordanian variant, based on Shir 1 (FV4030/2).

EXPORT VEHICLES BY COUNTRY

Country	Type and mark	Quantity delivered	Dates	Remarks
IRAQ	ARRV	29	c.1980	Plus c.200–300 MBT captured from Iran 1980–88, of which 90 gifted to Jordan 1990. 136 MBT captured from Kuwait 1990.
IRAN	MBT Mk 3/3P MBT Mk 5/1P MBT Mk 5/3P AVLB ARV	73 634 185 14 41	1971–73 1973–76 1976–78 c.1973–76 c.1973–76	Up to 300 MBT captured by Iraq of which 90 gifted to Jordan 1990. 8 × Mk 5/3P (FV4030/1) at MVEE in UK in 1979, so not delivered. 73 ordered, only 41 delivered.
JORDAN	Khalid ARV (J) AVLB MBT Mk 3 and 5	274 21 5 90	c.1981–present	Khalid based on FV4030/2. One ARV (J) gifted to Oman in 1981. c.21 ARRV gifted as part of al Hussein project 2002–05. Gifted by Iraq 1988.
KUWAIT	MBT Mk 5/2K	165	1976–80	Majority captured by Iraq in 1990.
OMAN	MBT Mk 7/2C MBT Mk 15 (Qayd al Ardh)	12 15	1981 1984–85	Leased from UK 1981–83, bought 1984. One ARV (J) gifted by Jordan in 1981.

Chapter Five

Chieftain variants

Chieftain was successfully developed into a number of specialised variants, including Armoured Vehicle Launched Bridge (AVLB), Armoured Recovery Vehicles (ARVs), and Armoured Vehicle Royal Engineers (AVRE), all of which added valuable capability to battlegroups, and which proved their worth when they were operated in the Gulf in 1991, the only time that Chieftain went to war under the British flag.

OPPOSITE Britain has always led the world in producing specialist armoured vehicles. The AVLB was one of a number of Chieftain-based variants used to support the field army; they proved to be useful vehicles, and were adopted not just in Britain but by a number of foreign armies as well. The No 8 bridge shown here could rapidly cross a gap of nearly 23m.

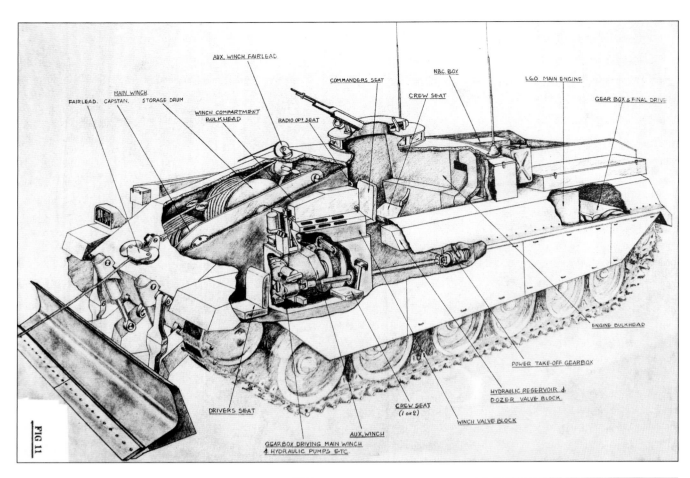

AUX. WINCH FAIRLEAD

MAIN WINCH.
FAIRLEAD. CAPSTAN. STORAGE DRUM

COMMANDERS SEAT

NBC BOX

L60 MAIN ENGINE

CREW SEAT

GEAR BOX & FINAL DRIVE

WINCH COMPARTMENT
BULKHEAD

RADIO OPt. SEAT

ENGINE BULKHEAD

POWER TAKE-OFF GEARBOX

HYDRAULIC RESERVOIR &
DOZER VALVE BLOCK

DRIVERS SEAT

CREW SEAT
(1 or 2)

WINCH VALVE BLOCK

AUX. WINCH

GEARBOX DRIVING MAIN WINCH
& HYDRAULIC PUMPS ETC

FIG 11

ABOVE A sketch from the mid-1960s showing the basic layout to be used for both the ARV and AEV (W). The location of the two winches within the hull front necessitated moving the driver to the left of the centreline. On the service ARV, both winches were located to the front right of the hull.

CENTRE AND RIGHT What FV4207 AEV (G) might have looked like – a bit of a Tankenstein's monster in terms of combining a lot of roles on one platform, but the version without the cumbersome A frame could have been a very useful item for the RE (and therefore the field army as a whole).

In-service Chieftain variants

Even whilst the basic MBT was still taking shape in 1960, the RE, quite rightly, were pushing for specialist versions to be made for their needs, which would replace the Centurion variants in service. Notes made at the time still referred to these as 'funnies', reflecting the Second World War experience of the officers involved. It made sense to design specialist vehicles that used the in-service MBT as their basis, as this would simplify production, training, and the supply of spare parts and fuel, as well as giving them very similar mobility and protection to the tanks that they were supporting.

Following feasibility studies in 1963, three engineer variants based on Chieftain were proposed by GSR 3116 of May 1965 (and subsequently 3308 of September 1966): two types of Armoured Engineer Vehicle (AEV) – the (W) or winch and the (G) or gun versions – plus an AVLB bridgelayer. These were intended to replace the Centurion variants then in service. Realising that it would be impossible for one vehicle to fulfil all the engineer roles required, the AEV was to have two distinct sub-types.

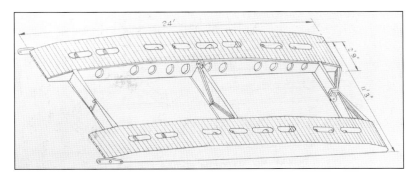

Fifteen FV4207 aka AEV (Gun) were required; these would retain the turret of Chieftain in order to mount the 165mm demolition gun, and might also be fitted with an A frame on the turret. In addition, 53 of the AEV (Winch) would be procured, which was to have the turret removed and replaced with a fixed superstructure very similar to that proposed for the ARV, but able to carry a 24ft No 7 twin-track bridge for crossing trenches and similar narrow obstacles, in place of the fascines that had been in use since the First World War. Although at first glance this seems like a ridiculously short bridge, studies had shown that 75% of water obstacles in north-west Europe could be crossed by its 20ft effective span. The tank would also mount a dozer blade, and the 30-ton winch would assist

ABOVE The 24ft-long No 7 bridge would have been able to span a 20ft gap, and its track width allowed it to carry a range of wheeled and tracked vehicles; the gap between the trackways could be filled with removable panels.

LEFT AEV (W)/ Chieftain AVRE prototype 03SP21 carrying the No 7 short-span bridge (upside down); neither entered service. In 1980 this vehicle was converted into Training ARV 00HB83.

it when exiting from obstacles and climbing steep banks. It was also to be used to act as an engineer command vehicle in forward areas. In 1967, the AEV (W) was renamed Chieftain AVRE and the AEV (G) was cancelled, meaning that the 165mm-armed Centurion AVREs would continue in service for another two decades.

FV4203 AVRE

By 1969 the design for the Chieftain AVRE had been completed and two ROFL prototypes (E1 03SP20 and E2 03SP21) with No 7 Class 60 bridges were on order. The hull of the prototype AVRE was the same as that used on the ARV being developed concurrently, and mounted a 30-ton winch plus a dozer blade/earth bucket. The bridge was carried upside down above the hull, and was launched in front of the vehicle using the up-and-over method. However, the decision was then made to stop developing both the AVRE and its No 7 bridge; this was because the Combat Engineer Tractor (CET) was being developed at Leeds, and it was realised that funds would not be available for both vehicles; thus in April 1969 the Chieftain AVRE project was stopped in favour of the CET (although development work was allowed to continue on the two prototypes, E1 and E2, in case the CET failed to live up to

expectations).[33] So it was that, by the end of the decade, both AEVs had been cancelled, leaving the AVLB as the sole Chieftain variant being developed for the engineers.

Luckily, this was not the end of the AVRE story. The RE were still keen on replacing their old petrol-engined Centurion Mk 5 AVREs, and the opportunity came about with the introduction of Chieftain's replacement, the Challenger 1, in the mid-1980s. It was realised that some Chieftain MBTs would shortly become surplus, and it was agreed that 13, later 17, Chieftains would be made available for conversion. As the new vehicle would be operating in support of the much more mobile Challenger, it was critical to ensure that the new vehicle had as good a power-to-weight ratio as possible. Therefore, it was decided that the turret would have to go (saving around 12 tons), which meant that the 165mm gun would not be able to be mounted as many had hoped. It could, however, be fitted with either a standard Chieftain dozer blade or a modified Centurion mine plough, could tow either two AVRE trailers or Giant Viper (GV) mine-clearance trailers, and would have a superstructure (known initially as the roof-rack but always called the hamper). The hamper could carry and lay three maxi pipe fascines or six rolls of Class 60 trackway. Six fixed legs welded to the hull supported the three sections of the hamper. The rear hamper was fixed, whereas the rear of the centre hamper, and the front of the forward hamper, could be raised and lowered by hydraulic rams to drop the fascines or trackway off the front of the vehicle. It was then decided that the tank should also be able to carry a No 9 tank bridge or other engineer stores, and rollers were mounted to the hamper to facilitate loading and unloading. (It could not launch a bridge; the intention was for the AVRE to be able to carry a spare bridge in support of an AVLB.) A seventh roll of trackway could also be carried on the hull rear if required. A Rotzler hydraulic winch was also fitted.

A wooden mock-up was made, followed by a functioning prototype; both vehicles used were AVLB Mk 2 hulls, which were adapted at Bovington in late 1984 and extensively trialled

BELOW AVRE carrying two pipe fascines and towing an AVRE trailer carrying Class 60 trackway.

33 As so often, cost was a major factor: each Chieftain AVRE would cost £100K, but CET was only £40K.

there. The design was then adapted for the Chieftain MBT hulls which were to be used for the conversions; in order to speed up the introduction into service it was decided that the conversions would be carried out by the army. Starting in February 1986, 17 Chieftain tanks were converted into AVREs at 21 Engineer base workshops in Willich, Germany, to the design of WO1 David Clegg RE, who was subsequently awarded the MBE for his work on the project. The first vehicle, No 1, was completed by mid-August 1986, and was immediately sent for trials to 32nd Armoured Engineer Regiment in BAOR in order to confirm the design before any other conversions were made. This was a sensible initiative, as around 40 modifications were incorporated on to No 2. No 3 followed suit, and the design was then frozen from No 4 onwards, to avoid having 17 different variants of the design in service. The last tank was completed by the end of 1987. Once converted they were given the designation AVRE Mk 6/2C and sometimes called the interim AVRE, but were usually known as the Willich AVREs. The AVREs had a crew of four: the driver and commander, and two additional crewmen who sat either side of the commander in very uncomfortable positions due to the low roof.

Sixteen of the tanks converted were Mk 2s, with a solitary Mk 1. Nine of the converted

AVREs went to 23rd Engineer Regiment, five to 32nd Armoured Engineer Regiment, two to BATUS and one to Bovington. It was estimated that the conversions were completed at a maximum of £80K each, which compared extremely favourably with an estimate of nearly five times that had industry completed the job. (Two more hulls were later converted at 23 base workshops in Wetter to fulfil a need for additional AVREs in BATUS; these were 00FD58 and 04EB85.)

Despite some problems with reliability – the tanks used were old and tired, the ones that the

ABOVE Using the Chieftain's on-board crane to load two rolls of trackway.

BELOW Launching the GV rocket mine-clearing device from behind AVRE 04EB85. Note that it is loaded with three rolls of pipe fascines, and is towing two GV trailers. *(TM 7431-081)*

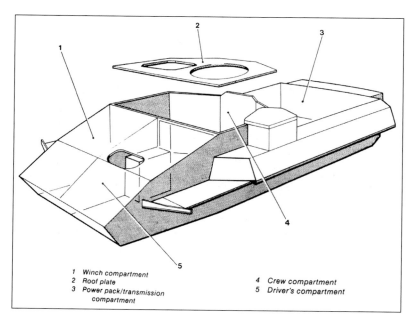

1 Winch compartment
2 Roof plate
3 Power pack/transmission compartment
4 Crew compartment
5 Driver's compartment

ABOVE The hull plates of the ARV, showing the removable roof with the second hatch added after trials.

RAC could most easily spare and had not been overhauled – the design gave the RE a vehicle that was capable of providing battlegroups with a whole range of close support engineer capabilities. Fourteen of the Willich AVREs were used in support of Operation GRANBY in the Gulf in 1991, where they received extra protection in the shape of four Warrior Explosive Reactive Armour (ERA) panels being fitted to either side of the crew compartment, together adding 1.2 tons to the vehicle. A net of chains were fitted, hanging from the hampers to detonate Ruchnoy Protivotankovy Granatomyot (aka rocket-propelled grenade – RPG) rounds, the ones at the front unpopular as they impeded the driver's vision.

In the Gulf they proved to be very useful, which reinforced the decision made in 1989 to convert more surplus hulls to AVREs; in late 1989, VDS were contracted to convert 48 more MBTs into AVREs. The design was very much based upon Clegg's, but improved in the light of experience, with a rear hydraulic hamper in addition to the front one, plus a crane for loading/unloading stores. Forty-six tanks plus two prototypes were converted at Elswick in two batches (30 and 16) between 1991 and late 1994. The new vehicle was generally referred to as Chieftain Armoured Vehicle Royal Engineers (CHAVRE). Once they were in service most of the Willich AVREs were retired, although a few soldiered on at Bovington as training vehicles.

FV4204 ARV

GSR 3308 was issued in 1966, covering the requirement not only for a Chieftain-based ARV, but also the AEV (W) and (R). As we have seen, the latter two were cancelled, leaving a stated requirement for 77 ARVs to be developed and built. ROFL was given a development contract in January 1967, but this was held up waiting for financial approval until October. Three prototypes were originally envisaged but this was reduced to two, trials beginning in late 1970 as soon as the first vehicle, R1, was delivered to MVEE on 3 December. Experience gained with R1 allowed many defects to be rectified whilst building the second, R2, which was ready in November 1972. Both vehicles were trialled not only at MVEE but also by the user, at the REME recovery school at Borden. Aside from major changes to the hydraulics, winches and earth anchor, it was decided that there should be a second hatch in the vehicle roof; the roof plate was removable to allow the winches to be changed when necessary. The vehicle required a crew of four: commander, driver/winchman, recovery mechanic and radio operator (usually, in reality, a vehicle mechanic). The commander was provided with a No 17 Mk 2 cupola, giving him all-round vision (when not impeded by equipment), and which mounted an L37 MG for local defence. Four banks of MBSGD were fitted, one on each corner. A No 4 NBC pack was fitted to the rear of the hull (which was also used on AVREs and AVLBs).

The main recovery equipment fitted was a 30-ton winch with a 3-ton auxiliary winch, driven from a power take-off (PTO) from the ME. Rigid tow bars were carried to allow MBTs to be towed a reasonable distance at speed. A 3.58m-wide dozer blade was mounted on the front that would also serve as a 90-ton earth anchor during winching operations. The ARV design based upon R2 was accepted in February 1973, and the vehicles were built at the VA factory at Elswick between June 1975 and May 1977 – it was necessary to go back to Vickers as ROFL was fully engaged in building MBTs and AVLBs for Iran. A production contract for 75 ARVs (74 for REME,

1 as an MVEE reference vehicle) was placed with Vickers on 13 June 1973 – in advance of the official acceptance – at a cost of £9.716 million. Deliveries began in mid-1975 and were completed two years later. A subsequent contract was then placed for a further 11 vehicles, which were built in May and June 1977, and finally one for three 'training' ARVs rebuilt from Special Projects (SP) vehicles in late 1980; two of these were AEV (W) prototypes E1 and E2, the other was R1, one of the two ARV prototypes.

The concept of an ARRV seems to have stemmed from a requirement for such a vehicle by the Iranians around 1974, in order to support the Shir 1 and 2 tanks it had on order; an order for up to 175 was considered although it is not certain if a contract was placed or for how many. Based upon the ARV

ABOVE A demonstration of the amazing capability of the dozer blade when used as an earth anchor, winching itself up by raw power. Such strength would make the Chieftain ARV a very useful recovery asset, and often meant that it was *the* priority equipment for repair, even before gun tanks.

BELOW The ARV driver's cab was very different to that used on the MBT, as the driver was also the winch and dozer blade operator.

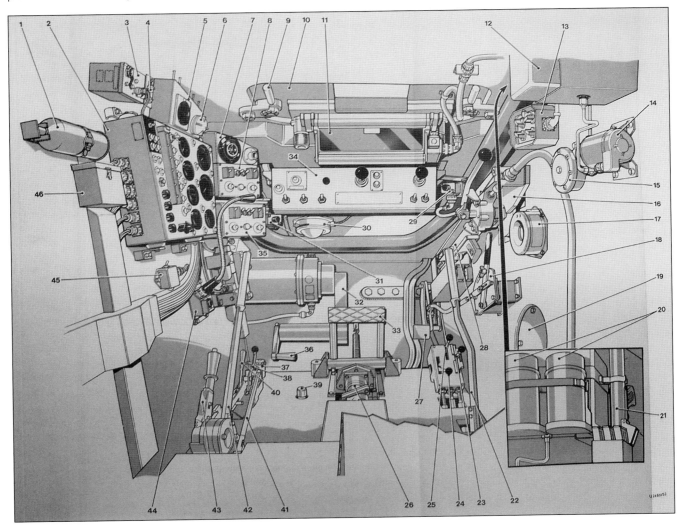

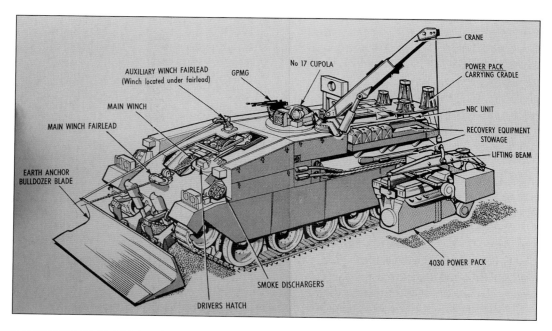

RIGHT A preliminary artist's impression of the ARRV (P) produced for Iranian approval in the mid-1970s, hence the CV12 (FV4030) powerpack illustrated.

CRANE

POWER PACK CARRYING CRADLE

NBC UNIT

RECOVERY EQUIPMENT STOWAGE

LIFTING BEAM

4030 POWER PACK

No 17 CUPOLA

GPMG

AUXILIARY WINCH FAIRLEAD
(Winch located under fairlead)

MAIN WINCH

MAIN WINCH FAIRLEAD

EARTH ANCHOR BULLDOZER BLADE

DRIVERS HATCH

SMOKE DISCHARGERS

ABOVE AND BELOW ... and the actual vehicle, also carrying a CV12. The high silhouette when carrying a powerpack was much criticised on tactical grounds.

and known as ARRV (P),[34] a prototype was built using a 5-ton commercial crane fitted to the left rear to allow the crew to lift and change major assemblies as well as carrying out recovery tasks. Additionally, a carrying cradle was mounted above the rear decks capable of carrying either an L60 or CV12 (Shir/Challenger) powerpack, or indeed other smaller assemblies. The idea was for the ARRV to carry a new pack to the site of a vehicle casualty, and there be able to swap the packs over and then return the unserviceable pack to a powerpack repair facility for rectification. The vehicle, when carrying a powerpack, looked enormously high and attracted a great deal of criticism from British officers on tactical grounds – the critics failed to note that it was still over 2ft lower than an AVLB carrying a bridge or an AVRE carrying fascines.

Then came the fall of the Shah, so Vickers found itself in the same situation as that in Leeds – a full order book from a customer who, for political reasons, could not be supplied with the vehicles, and a factory tooled-up and full of components and raw materials. Luckily for Vickers, the decision to turn FV4030/3 into Challenger (see Haynes Manual *Challenger 1 Main Battle Tank* for details) led to an investigation into suitable support vehicles, where it was realised very

34 P for Persian.

quickly that the FV434 REME vehicle could not lift the powerpack on Challenger, and that the Chieftain ARRV would be a better solution for the Challenger units until a bespoke solution could be brought into service.[35] The ARRV (P) designed for Iran was therefore dusted off and given a 6.5-ton Atlas crane,[36] emerging as the Chieftain ARRV Mk 7, and two early conversions supported the first Challenger 1 regiment, the Royal Hussars (RH), on Exercise SPEARPOINT in 1984; the conversion programme lasted from 1983 until 1989 with 69 tanks, the majority of the ARV fleet, being converted. The Chieftain ARRV was renamed CHARRV when the Challenger version known as CRARRV came into service in the early 1990s. In many ways the introduction of the ARRV into British service mirrored that of the Challenger tank: the Iranians had a requirement which was developed for them; the British wanted something similar but could not afford it; the Iranian revolution prevented the vehicle being supplied; and the British then completed development and brought the vehicle into service themselves.

In 1996 Britain conducted an inquiry into the supply of weapons to the Saddam Hussein regime in Iraq. During the investigation it was reported that, after Britain had 'absorbed' about 50 ARVs from a cancelled Iranian order, it was still left with another 50 in an incomplete state and with no buyer.[37] The MoD authorised their completion whilst efforts were made to find an export outlet. In November 1979, 21 ARRVs were ordered by Jordan to support their purchase of Khalid tanks, leaving 29 still

ABOVE The ARRV from the rear, giving a good impression of the amount of recovery equipment carried on the hull.

CENTRE This ARRV is carrying not only an L60 engine but also a TN12 gearbox.

RIGHT One of the trial vehicles with the CV12 powerpack alongside. The closer to the vehicle the pack was, the more weight could be lifted by the Atlas crane.

---

35 This was fortunate for Vickers, as each ARV built at Elswick cost £7.7K more than if it had been built at ROFL, but capacity at Leeds was full.

36 Reduced to 4.3 tons at full extension.

37 As there is no record of these 50 ARVs entering British Army service, it must be assumed that either they were able to be subsumed into the FV15998 contract, or that a foreign buyer was found for them. The 29 ARRVs that went to Iraq in 1980 seem to have come from this source.

ABOVE An ARRV
towing an AVRE –
backwards – complete
with fascines and
trackway. The ARRV
crew have, in typical
style, constructed a
'penthouse' over the
engine decks.

needing a buyer.[38] Iraq then expressed an interest in them but, in order to keep the sale out of the public eye, it was agreed by the three countries involved that Jordan would act as purchaser for them, and that Iraq would then pay for and receive the vehicles from Jordan. Jordan did the right thing in terms of the contract, by requesting, and receiving, permission for the transfer from the Minister of State in the MoD. Spares support was dealt with in a similar manner, but when the first request was received in 1985, the security section of the MoD became involved. Firstly, they did not even know that Iraq had obtained the ARRVs, and, secondly, they objected on the grounds that the spares could be used to repair the MBTs held by Iraq – at the time it was assessed that Iraq was holding around 150 captured from Iran. Therefore, the only spares authorised were those which could not be used on MBTs.

The majority of the UK ARV fleet was converted by various REME workshops to become ARRVs: at least 69 were converted between 1982 and 1988. They were rendered

38 These were known as ARV (J), the J standing for Jordan. Because an ARRV for Iran had already been designed, the design was refined and then put into production, with the first Jordanian vehicles, 06SP26 and 27, being trialled in 1980.

obsolete by the introduction into service of the CRARRV and were phased out. At least 21 of the surplus ARRVs and a couple of (apparently still unconverted) ARVs were supplied to Jordan as part of the Al Hussein Challenger 1 gift between 2002 and 2005. In 1992, with both CHARRV and CRARRV in service, a competition to give both vehicles names was undertaken, open to military personnel. CRARRV was won by the suggestion Rhino, and CHARRV by the unlikely name of Reclaimer: it is probable that the REME, the operator of the vehicles, wanted their fleet to all have names beginning with the letter R. Neither name really stuck, though, and the author has no recollection of either being used.

FV4205 AVLB

In 1946, studies had revealed that the maximum length of a bridge that could be carried on an AFV was 52ft – any longer and the vehicle would be unable to manoeuvre in close country, towns and so on. This information was used when designing the new bridge to be carried on the Chieftain AVLB, later named the No 8 bridge. This was a folding design to reduce the length when being

transported, hinged in the middle and with a length when folded of 40ft. When deployed, it would be 80ft long and capable of bridging an obstacle with a maximum 75ft span; it weighed about 12 tons. Design of the carrying vehicle based upon Chieftain started in 1962; the MBT glacis was replaced with a special larger casting made for the bridge launching mechanism and commander's hatch, and welded to the top rear of the hull was the bridge support structure. The driver occupied the normal position in the front centre; both the commander and third crewman, the radio operator, used the commander's hatch to enter the central compartment; and a fourth crewman could be carried if necessary.

In order to prove the concept before starting series production, four vehicles, known as AVLB Mk 2 prototypes were built. These were completed in November 1968 at Leeds, and took the registration numbers 00FB01–04; during the trials they were referred to as prototypes P1–P4. Extensive troop trials took place in BAOR between January and June 1969 using 00FB04, during which time its bridge was laid and recovered 138 times, and crossed by no less than 522 vehicles, including 427 MBT. The bridgelayers were manned by

soldiers from 2RTR, as no RE were then trained on Chieftains. Following these and other trials, the vehicle and bridge design was accepted in 1971, with the No 8 bridge being made by Vickers in Elswick, and the bridgelayers being a joint project: the vehicle hulls were built

ABOVE An ARRV belonging to 1RTR driving with the jib partially extended.

BELOW The hull of AVLB Mk 2 prototype P3 being used as a driver training tank (known locally as a Wedge) at Bovington in 2006. This was one of the two hulls that were used to test the AVRE concept at Bovington in 1984 prior to the Willich AVREs being built, and still carries some of the fittings and modifications.

ABOVE A Chieftain Mk 5 AVLB carrying a No 8 scissors tank bridge. *(Courtesy Andy Brend)*

BELOW The 44ft No 9 bridge could also be carried; although shorter in gap-crossing ability than the No 8, as a single-span design overall it made the vehicle 4ft longer. *(Courtesy Andy Brend)*

BELOW The launching mechanism shown resting on the ground without a bridge mounted – the effect on the driver's visibility can be imagined.

at ROFL, but the superstructure work was supplied by ROF Nottingham.

Production of the bespoke AVLB Mk 5 based upon the Mk 5 MBT was undertaken at Leeds between June 1973 and March 1977, with 37 being built for the British Army. (A further 14 were built for Iran in the same period, and five more for Jordan in the 1980s.) Deployment to BAOR started in 1974. It was then decided in March 1984 that more were required. Following trials in 1985, 11 surplus Mk 1/4 tanks were upgraded and converted to AVLB Mk 6s by Vickers at a cost of £4.5 million, with the first three vehicles delivered in June 1986, and the final one four months later. As these tanks had the original MBT glacis, the hole left by the removal of the turret was closed off with a 19mm plate incorporating the commander's hatch and periscopes.

Using the scissors method, the No 8 bridge is hydraulically launched in three stages. Firstly, the bridge is pushed forwards and downwards until the rollers on the nose contact the ground just in front of the launch vehicle. Next, the front/forward half of the bridge pivots open with a scissors action, moving forward and downwards until the far toe contacts the ground on the other side of the obstacle. The bridge can now lock together with the centre hinge fully closed, allowing the launch vehicle to disengage and move away from – or over – the bridge. The whole operation takes about three minutes with the crew remaining under armour, and the bridge can be recovered in about ten minutes from either side, although crewmen are required to dismount for this in order to connect up. The shorter No 9 bridge could also be launched from the AVLB using the same mechanism with an up-and-over method. This was a single span (non-hinged) bridge with an overall length of 44ft, and so was capable of crossing a 40ft gap. It was approved for service in 1974 but for production reasons did not enter service until 1978. Towards the end of its life a range of newer bridges were built that could also be used on the AVLB; these included the Nos 10 (24.5m), 11 (14.5m) and 12 (12m).

In 1984, the Royal Army Ordnance Corps asked the RAC to decide whether it wanted to retain the ten Chieftain turrets that were in storage at the Central Ordnance Depot,

ABOVE An AVLB driving forward to recover a bridge during a demonstration at Bovington. *(Courtesy Andy Brend)*

BELOW Two AVLBs, the nearest one carrying a No 9 'up-and-over' bridge, whilst the farthest carries the longer No 8 scissors bridge.

ABOVE Stages of the launch sequence, taken from an official publication.

BELOW AND RIGHT Overbridging: the first bridge had only partially covered the gap, so a second bridge is being laid to overlap it and complete the task.

RIGHT A Chieftain AVLB in Saudi Arabia in 1991, just prior to the start of hostilities. It has been up-armoured with Warrior side packs and anti-RPG chains across the front. Multi-tasking the RE tanks made them more flexible as they could conduct a number of roles.

Bicester; presumably some of these were the ones removed from the vehicles converted to AVLBs, plus others including possibly from the Willich AVREs. They were heavy and took up valuable space, and, although it is not clear what happened, it is probable that they were scrapped, although some may have found their way to MVEE to be used as the basis for Windsor trial turrets.

Chieftain goes to war (at last)

In 1990 when 7 Armoured Brigade, and subsequently 1st Armoured Division, deployed to Saudi Arabia as part of Operation DESERT SHIELD, Chieftain went with them. The MBTs used were all Challenger 1s, but the RE and REME took a number of Chieftain (Willich)

VARIANT CHARACTERISTICS

	AVLB Mk 5	AVRE Mk 6/2	ARV Mk 5	ARRV Mk 7
Eqpt code	0422-2050	0300-3762	0505-2050	0505-3003
Weight unladen lb	90,610lb	111,444lb	114,240lb	122,683lb (laden)
Bridge class laden	60 (with No 8 bridge). 45 (unladen)	70	60	60
Height overall	N/A	8' 4"	8' 10" (cupola)	9' 3"
Height maximum	13'8" (No 8 bridge)	13' 9" (fascine)	9' 2"	11'4" (carrying L60)
Length maximum	45' 1"	33' 3"	28' 5"	28' 2"
Width overall	13' 8" (with No 8 or No 9 bridge)	13' 11"	11' 7"	11' 7"
Ground clearance	23"	24" front, 19" rear	23"	20" front, 23" rear
L60	Mk 7A	Mk 13A	Mk 7A 720bhp	Mk 14A 720bhp
H30	Mk 10A			
Max speed	26.6mph	26.5mph	26.6mph	26.4mph
Max speed reverse	6.11mph			
Comd's day sight	N/A	AV No 2100 Mk 31	No 62 or 64	No 62
Comd's night sight	N/A		No 64	L7A1
Comd's periscopes	6 × No 39	6 × No 40 Mk 2	7 × No 40 Mk 2	
Dvr's day sight	No 36		No 45	
Dvr's night sight	L4A1			L11A1

Source: technical handbooks.

LEFT **A REME ARRV conducts a CV12 pack lift on a Challenger. The inability of Chieftain ARRVs to properly support the Challenger regiments led to the emergency deployment of CRARRV. The items on the 120mm barrel are sleeping bags.**

AVREs, AVLBs and ARRVs to support the armoured troops. The 21st Engineer and 32nd Armoured Engineer Regiment crewed the AVREs and AVLBs, whilst the REME ARVs supported the Challenger regiments (supplemented by the rapid deployment of the first Challenger-based CRARRVs) as well as the RE tanks. Thus, 25 years after it entered service, Chieftain finally saw combat under the union flag.

Tank dozer

A tank dozer system for Chieftain had been initially fitted to prototype P4, and was then trialled on 02EB56 between October and December 1966 where it was found to be successful. All MBTs were built able to take the dozer kit, with a mounting bracket forward of the driver's position and an electrical PTO (sealed for NBC conditions) mounted on the right-hand hull side. The right-hand front stowage bin was removed and replaced by a similar-sized box containing the electro-hydraulic power unit, with an oil reservoir and pump unit, with the control box and joystick mounted inside the driver's cab to the RHS. The main body of the blade was made of aluminium for lightness, with a steel cutting edge for strength. It was 12ft 6in wide, 6in wider than the basic vehicle, and weighed 2,700lb, adding about 1 ton to the overall weight. The bridge class with the dozer fitted was 60 rather than the normal 56. Each armoured squadron normally had one on strength, with some units

ABOVE One of the Willich AVREs carrying a relatively light load of only two pipe fascines; the AVREs were expected to be critical in overcoming Iraqi-prepared defensive positions.

BELOW The dozer attachment in the down position, ready for work. This tank is also shown in Chapter Four, being prepared for destruction.

preferring to keep it in SHQ, others choosing
to fit it to one of the troop corporal's tanks.
When using tank transporters, dozer tanks had
to be reversed on to the trailer, an even trickier
operation than with normal gun tanks.

Training equipment

A variety of simulators known as Classroom
Instructional Mountings (CIMs) were
ordered early in Chieftain's development to
assist in training on the most complicated
vehicle that the RAC had ever operated.
Made by Wharton of Elstree, as well as turret
CIMs made for the REME for training their
tradesmen, gunnery CIMs were received
by the gunnery establishments and all the
regiments. These were, in effect, replica cutaway turrets, allowing hydraulically controlled
firing simulation, in order for soldiers to
practise loading the 120mm gun, as well as
experience stoppages and misfire drills on all
weapon systems. Maintenance could also be
demonstrated on them, and additionally they
could be used to mount the Field Miniature
Range (FMR) .22in gunnery simulator. Gunnery
CIMs cost £34K each in February 1964,
with the driving simulator (see below) costing
around £27.5K. Although extremely useful,
one of the problems not anticipated with
such training aids was the need to keep them
modified to reflect accurately the tanks that
they were replicating, which proved to be a
time-consuming and costly exercise, due to the
amount of modifications made to the tank.

To speed up (and lower the cost of) driver
training, the D&M School at Bovington was

LEFT The REME version of the CIM, used to train Electrical Control Technicians, or ECEs for short. All the electrical systems are replicated, including the Light Projector, but the gun could not recoil – the large cylinder on the muzzle is a counterweight. Notice the cutaway hull alongside.
(Courtesy Jonathan Falconer)

BELOW The terrain model used with the driving simulator.
(TM 5163B4)

supplied with a Link-Miles driver trainer. This comprised: a replica driver's compartment with a TV screen on the top which the student viewed through his periscope; an instructor's console; a computer; a landscape model measuring 30ft × 12ft; and a moving gantry above the model with a TV camera mounted on it. The model represented 1.3 square miles of varied terrain, and as the student drove around a route ordered by the instructor, the gantry moved so that the camera transmitted a picture replicating the driver's view. The Treasury, in its inimitable way, questioned the need for the driver trainer after a publicity film

for Chieftain claimed that it was so simple that 'even a girl could drive it'.

Tactical engagement simulation

During the life of the tank, it was fitted with three different tactical engagement simulation systems. Although they differed a lot in terms of the technology used and the realism achieved, they all sought to allow 'force on force' training to take place, by replicating firing and being hit. A downside of all three systems was that they required the crews to fit any number of additional boxes, linked by dozens of cables, to their tanks. This was never a popular task, as the boxes reduced stowage and room inside the tank, and the cables had to be carefully routed to prevent them becoming snagged or presenting a trip hazard. Additionally, reliability was a problem and the systems, once installed, all required careful setting up and calibration. However, when installed correctly – particularly applicable to the Direct Fire Weapons Effects Simulator (DFWES) – they provided the crews with excellent training, notably from 1995 at BATUS where an Opposing Force (OPFOR) used surrogate vehicles to play a realistic and thinking enemy, so much better than an umpire with a white armband.

LEFT If hit and knocked out, a smoke generator would be fired, the billowing orange smoke announcing the kill to the world.

BELOW One of the retro-reflector units used with DFWES, the latest generation of weapons effects simulators used on Chieftain.

In chronological order, the systems used were called Fire Simulator (SIMFIRE), Fire Simulator (IFCS) (SIMFICS) and DFWES. Each allowed the tank to simulate firing at another, with a pyrotechnic device to indicate that the MA had been fired; these were often referred to as flash-bangs. If hit (or near-missed) by another tank, the equipment would give the crew a warning, and if 'killed', an orange smoke generator would be initiated, indicating the fact not only to the crew but also to the attacker. Space precludes going into detail of each system, but careful scrutiny of the images elsewhere in this book will reveal many examples of the systems in use.

LEFT A DFWES-equipped Mk 11, showing the laser projector fitted within the muzzle, as well as other components, including the sound simulator speaker fitted above the MBSGD.

Chapter Six

Trials and funnies

As well as the variants already detailed, Chieftain was used as the basis for a number of interesting and imaginative trials, including deep-wading, remote-control and even a fire-suppression vehicle. Most of these did not enter service, but they provided invaluable research data for the next generation of tanks.

OPPOSITE FVRDE and its successor MVEE were heavily involved in dozens – if not hundreds – of trials involving the Chieftain. Some were intended to improve the tank in service; others just used the tank as a convenient platform for developmental and conceptual trials. *(Courtesy M.P. Robinson)*

137

RIGHT Mk 4 tank 02SP97 ended up being converted to a tracked crane for assistance with heavy trials work. Note the adjusted suspension unit spacing necessary with the hull modifications.

Trials

Trials are an integral part of the development process and are used to test concepts to see whether they work as intended, when faced with realistic conditions (and crews). The British Army operated (and still does) a special unit to conduct such tests, known as ATDU, based in Bovington. Heavily involved in the testing of prototype Chieftains in its earlier guise as the RAC ETW, the successor ATDU was central to the majority of the improvements and enhancements made to Chieftain throughout its long service, although some such trials were conducted by normal regiments, and many were intended to support export drives.

One of these was Exercise DRYFOOT, which took place at the Yuma Proving Ground, Arizona, in mid-1971 and was conducted not by ATDU but by crews from two cavalry regiments. Two Chieftains were used, 02SP96 and 97; the former was described as the 'Automotive tank' and the latter the 'NBC tank'. These were the two Mk 4 tanks originally modified for the Israelis, and followed on from the important work on dust mitigation conducted at the insistence of General Tal. The trials deliberately

made conditions as dusty as possible by driving for hours in the dust clouds of the tank in front, hence the choice of location. Dust sampling was conducted from a number of points: the NBC air inlet, the front left fuel filler cap, the engine compartment, inside the turret, the turret roof and the front hull by the RH headlamp. A large control box was mounted above the No 37 sight on the cupola. A new (No 3) NBC pack was also tested, which was not brought into service but which used the larger armoured box subsequently adopted to house the service No 6 pack, based upon the No 3.

We will now look at eight other examples of the types of trials carried out, which should give a fair impression of the whacky world of experimentation and improvement:

■ When Chieftain was introduced into the often freezing north German winter, the crews complained of the cold conditions inside the tank, and, as a result, crew heaters were periodically trialled throughout its life. The initial attempts involved the 17/21L to test a number of options in the winter of 1967/68. These were encouraging, although the poor old driver had the least effective heater, particularly when his hatch was open. (A driver's windscreen was originally envisaged for the tank, but despite being trialled in BAOR it never entered service.) However, nothing was brought into service. By the early 1980s wiring looms for heated crew oversuits had been fitted to most vehicles, and although in 1984 Raychem Ltd proposed a design of such suits (known as ITCH or Individual Tank Crewman's Heater), they were not introduced. And so it went on; a successful heating system was never fitted to Chieftain – mainly because the budgeteers decided that the 'retrofit costs were prohibitive'. (Perhaps it was something to do with Chieftain being designed for the Cold War? Boom Boom!) The author vividly remembers exercising in tanks with ice on the inside of the turrets, and training exercises at –20° and colder in Germany and BATUS that were often more about survival than tactical training. I have known gunners who spent the whole of an exercise period inside their sleeping bag in their seats, a luxury the other three crew members could not replicate.

- As Chieftain was entering service, a couple of Centurions were drowned in an accident involving landing craft. The inquiry revealed that Centurion had not had its centre of gravity (CoG) correctly revised since it was first introduced, despite numerous modifications and additional weight. It was necessary therefore to remedy this, and the opportunity was taken at the same time to work out the CoG for Chieftain. The only cranes large enough to lift the tanks off the ground were to be found in ports, and so a Chieftain and a late-mark Centurion were taken to the Royal Navy dockyard at Devonport, where they were suspended from their lifting eyes, allowing scientists to use surveying equipment to work out the exact CoG for both tanks.

- In 1965, a paper feasibility project was undertaken to examine the possibility of mounting the 'compact turret' from an American M60A2 tank, with its 152mm gun capable of firing 'Shillelagh missiles', on to a Chieftain hull. Presumably this was to give Chieftain an Anti-Tank Guided Weapon (ATGW) capability, although it will be recalled

ABOVE AND BELOW The centre of gravity experiment held at RN Base Devonport. The white lines on the bazooka plates assisted the scientists in measuring angles.

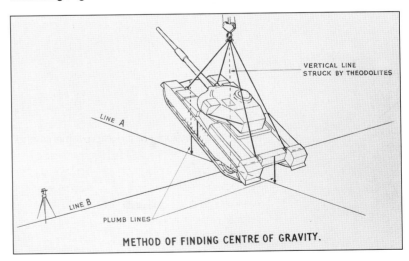

that there had been an intention to mount the British Swingfire system on to the tank until it had been cancelled the previous year. The new proposal was adjudged to be technically too difficult, but was reminiscent of the proposals around 1956 to build FV4201 hulls in such a way that they could, if required, mount American T95 tank turrets with a 90mm gun, which was happily abandoned when the USA stopped development of the tank.

■ Between December 1968 and July 1970, 02EB19 was trialled at FVRDE with US-designed T127E3 track, covering 2,784 miles in this time. This 24in track required special sprockets and idlers to be fitted, and was hoped to provide longer life than the in-service track. However good it was as track, it proved to be too heavy, adding (yet) another 550kg to the tank's weight, and thus did not proceed.

■ On 11 July 1980 the 5th Inniskilling Dragoon Guards supplied 18 Chieftains for a unique trial. The tanks were lined up almost 'shoulder to shoulder' in a line, positioned 50m outside and facing a rectangular artillery concentration box that measured 100 × 150m. The following HE shells were then fired into the box: 750 × 105mm, 660 × 155mm and 40 × 203mm, and the damage to the tanks was then assessed. Although there was much superficial damage – as might be expected after 1,450 shells had landed no further than 200m away – not one of the tanks was put out of action and they would have been able to continue to fight. Much interesting information was gained for the experimental community, but one can only sympathise for the crews from the Skins who had to repair their damaged vehicles afterwards.

■ In 1982, a series of trials took place to see whether it was feasible for a turret to be changed in the field, simulating taking a good turret off a damaged hull in order to put it on to a serviceable hull with a damaged turret. A crane (or cranes) with at least a 20-ton lift capacity was required to lift a 16,485kg turret complete with gun, cupola, Light Projector and all other items, but it was found to be possible, taking around 8hrs. This impressive task was then used as a demonstration of REME field repairs at the annual Staff College demonstration, held in Sennelager.

BELOW A turret lift demonstration. With the gun and all systems still fitted, the total weight was over 16 tons. *(Courtesy Andrew Chapman)*

In 1988, the Berlin Armoured Squadron identified a requirement for greater ammunition stowage for the commander's MG, as a result of the increased use it was expected to be put to in urban fighting; subsequently, a curved 1,000-round 'banana bin' was designed to replace the standard single box of 200 rounds.

A collaboration between ROFL and Air Log Ltd developed a new suspension system known as Hydrostrut, or HSS. Intended to improve the ride beyond that possible with Horstmann units, HSS was designed to be a one-for-one replacement for the standard suspension on Chieftain, by simply unbolting each Horstmann unit and replacing it with the new type. It had the advantage that each roadwheel was independently sprung, and shock was both absorbed and damped using a gas-pressure tube, mounted almost vertically. It was regularly tested by ATDU a number of times throughout the 1980s, starting in 1984. The report on its fitting to Mk 10 04EB40 in 1988 concluded that it gave a smoother ride as well as improved and faster cross-country mobility. The latter was important, as not only would the tank be able to move tactically quicker and thus expose itself less to enemy observation and fire, but this would also make shooting on the move more accurate. HSS was never fitted to service tanks, partly because it took so long to get into a serviceable and reliable state, but mainly because the replacement of the whole Chieftain fleet rendered it unnecessary.

ABOVE A predecessor to the Hydrogas system used on Challenger, the Hydrostrut system trialled on Chieftain could replace the existing Horstmann unit and give the crews a better ride, which made shooting on the move more accurate. It showed promise but did not come into service.

Chieftain 'funnies'

Chieftain became the test-bed vehicle for any number of experiments. Some of these were done specifically with Chieftain in mind, whereas many simply used it as a convenient test-bed; because of this, some of the Chieftains, on the strength of Chertsey, were used for any number of different trials, and can be regarded as some of the most important individual tanks in service. Space precludes detailing all of these, and in any case some of the research material remains secret. We can,

BELOW Tank 02SP85 shown in its normal guise as a Mk 3 MBT. Some of the SP tanks were converted many times during their lives as trial vehicles. *(Courtesy Brian Clark)*

LEFT Tank 02SP86, heavily modified and instrumented for a firing trial – note how nose-heavy the tank is, resting on its front suspension. *(Courtesy M.P. Robinson)*

CENTRE In early 1987, SP tank 06SP57 was modified from an old Mk 1/4 by fitting a GT601 gas turbine engine, which necessitated major alterations to the rear hull. This was not an attempt to improve mobility in Chieftain; it simply used Chieftain as a 'technology demonstrator' in order to study that type of engine.

however, take a peek behind the curtain of secrecy to conclude this work with a look at some of the interesting and unusual offspring of Chieftain used in such trials. The tanks used were often seen with an SP registration. Although MVEE was provided with a few Chieftains as permanent reference vehicles, most of the SP tanks were service vehicles loaned from the army. The following list is probably incomplete, but provides at least some of the tanks involved:

02SP85–86	Chieftain MBT Mk 3
02SP96–97	Chieftain Mk 4
03SP01–02	Chieftain MBT Mk 3/3
03SP06	Chieftain MBT Mk 3
03SP12–16	Chieftain MBT Mk 3
03SP18–21	Chieftain ARV
05SP30	Chieftain ARRV
05SP50	Khalid
05SP73	Chieftain MBT Mk 1
06SP26–27	Chieftain ARV
06SP49	Chieftain MBT Mk 5
06SP50	Chieftain MBT Mk 3 (G)
06SP51–53	Chieftain MBT Mk 1
06SP57–58	Chieftain MBT Mk 1/4
06SP71	Chieftain MBT Mk 5
06SP78	Chieftain MBT Mk 5

LEFT SPR4, aka 02EB45, with a weighted trials turret and additional ballast mounted on the hull. *(TM 6010D5)*

ABOVE The hull of 00FD66 fitted with the FV4030/3 Shir 2 turret T7. *(TM 7805B1)*

RIGHT Tank 05FA90 fitted with a 'pusher bar' to allow it to be assisted from behind when mine ploughing, 1992. *(TM 4224D1)*

BELOW The GBT 155R Universal SPG turret on Chieftain hull 00EB64 at the British Army Equipment Exhibition (BAEE), 1986. *(TM 1236D6)*

RIGHT Tank 04SP29 was the so-called 'JagdChieftain', a self-propelled gun project fitted with a dummy gun. Had the project been progressed, it would have been armoured using Chobham. *(TM 3546C1)*

Concept test rig aka JagdChieftain

In 1972, Britain and the Federal Republic of Germany embarked on a collaborative project to study turretless and fixed gun AFVs. MVEE took the lead on investigating a Chieftain hull fitted with a semi-fixed gun; the gun would be able to elevate or depress, but would be laid for line by moving the whole of the vehicle by its hydrostatic steering. The intention was to lighten the tank to around 35 tons, and reduce the crew to three; in many ways it mimicked the Swedish Strv 103 (S-Tank). By 1974, a prototype (04SP29) had been produced, known (as many similar projects were) as a CTR or Concept Test Rig. It was often informally called JagdChieftain, reflecting not only the

collaboration with the Germans but more specifically referring to similar German AFVs used in the Second World War. The trials tank was both ballasted and fitted with a dummy gun, but as so often, despite useful data being gathered, it was not proceeded with.

Chieftains 800 and 900

Chieftain 800 was the name given to official proposals to re-engine Chieftain with the smaller 800bhp CV8 version of the Rolls-Royce Condor, the 1,200bhp CV12 version of which was used on Khalid and Challenger. Two ex-Iranian Chieftains were converted in the late 1970s; these were two of the Mk 5/3P tanks that were never delivered, and used a fully automatic version of the TN12 Mk 5 gearbox. The new

RIGHT The dimensions of the CTR, shown without the dummy gun but with ballast on the nose to make up the weight of both the gun and the Chobham armour. This plan shows a full-length hull.

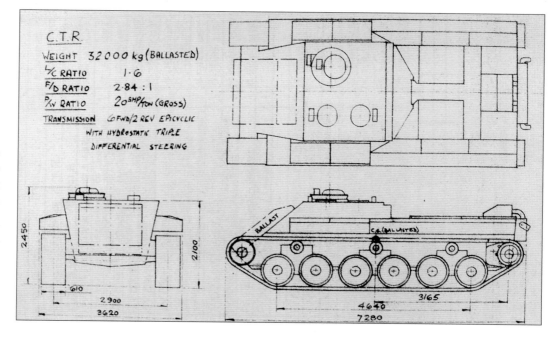

engine would have provided a little extra power but, more importantly, increased reliability – by the summer of 1979 one of the tanks had already clocked up 4,000 relatively trouble-free kilometres. One of the tanks was given the military sales registration 56MS09, but this was the only clue as to its identity as externally it was identical to a normal Mk 5 gun tank.

Although the title sounds similar, Chieftain 900 was a private venture by ROF, dating to 1981. Two prototypes were completed at Leeds in April 1982, and were shown at the British Army Equipment Exhibition of that summer. The intention was to demonstrate that Chieftain could have its mobility (and of course reliability) improved with a new powerpack, and that the turret and hull could be modified to be fitted with Chobham armour. In order to do the former, a Rolls-Royce Condor 900E engine was used, giving 900bhp at 2,300rpm, which increased the power-to-weight ratio to 18, and it was even suggested that this could be increased by another 100bhp, giving an even more impressive 20bhp per ton. The normal Chieftain TN12 gearbox was still used, but, as on Khalid, the Horstmann suspension units had nearly twice the wheel travel of the standard tank, allowing better use to be made of the extra power; this was sometimes referred to as 'Super Horstmann'. A cosmetic panel system, which, on a service tank, would conceal Chobham, was fitted to the turret and hull front and sides. Another innovative idea was to allow the customer a menu of options, including: HSS; solid-state Gun Control Equipment (GCE); Archer digital radios; APFSDS; thermal sights; air conditioning; and a laser warning system. Despite the attractiveness of many of these features, their addition was seen for what it was – an attempt to upgrade an ageing design and not a genuine modern tank, and so attracted no buyers.

Chieftain 2000

Tank 03EB35 was loaned to General Electric Company (GEC) Marconi in Chelmsford in 1993 in order to allow the company to test out their Centaur fire control system in a real tank; the turret from Chieftain 900 was mounted on to the standard hull and which was then known, rather grandly and optimistically, as Chieftain 2000.

ABOVE Tank 53MS09 – Chieftain 900, an attempt to update Chieftain for export markets. *(Courtesy Andy Brend)*

ABOVE The so-called GEC Marconi Chieftain 2000 shown in 1993, with additional armour on the turret front and sides from the Chieftain 900 project, and a panoramic commander's sight. *(TM 4633D5)*

BELOW When is a Chieftain not a Chieftain? Answer: when it is fitted with an experimental Marconi turret and a modified hull. *(TM 3819C5)*

Marksman and Sabre

Marksman was an air defence turret designed by VDS, and equipped with 2 × 35mm Oerlikon cannons. Electronics were supplied by Marconi, and the turret was mounted not only on Chieftain (53MS28) but on a number of other MBT hulls in order to demonstrate its versatility.

Chieftain Sabre was another proposed anti-aircraft tank, with the hull mounting an ROF/Thomson-CSF turret with two Oerlikon 30mm cannon; capable of firing 1,300 rounds per minute, the ammunition supply of 600 rounds

would last for less than 30 seconds. Although it was hoped for export orders (the British Army was not interested as its doctrine was based upon missile air defence), none were sold.

Water crossing

The British Army have been interested in developing techniques for crossing water obstacles in AVs for almost as long as the vehicles have existed. A number of techniques have been used on Chieftain, including fording, deep-wading and snorkelling. The tank is designed to be able to ford 1.07m without any special preparation. Deep-wading could about double this, but required extensive preparation in the form of sealing the hull and turret ring, as well as providing for engine intake and exhaust; it also required nerves of steel on the part of the driver.

Underwater-crossing equipment with a snorkel was trialled using a remote-control driving system between 1968 and 1972. The remote-control system was designed by Maj Dudley RTR at ETW Bovington, and allowed water-crossing trials to be conducted without putting a crew at risk should a problem occur. In order to seal the turret, because the entire vehicle would be submerged, a rubberised

LEFT So that is what those two hooks on the side of the hull were for! Tank 02EB63 rigged up for snorkelling trials, complete with the sealing kit covering the turret and rear hull. The same tank was used for Maj Dudley's remote-control experiments. *(TM 10059-003)*

wading kit was developed to seal the whole area – hence the presence of the wading rail on the top of the hull. As snorkelling was only ever experimented with, and never formed part of official doctrine, it is hard to understand why the extra weight this added was tolerated; indeed, the Kuwaitis dispensed with it when they bought their fleet of Chieftains.

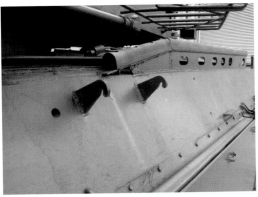

LEFT The two mysterious hooks on the hull side were fitted to support the bottom of the snorkel tower ladder but were otherwise superfluous.

BELOW Tank 02EB99 photographed partway through the Dri-Clad process.

Dri-Clad

The Dri-Clad system was designed to keep tanks that were required to be placed in long-term storage, particularly the WMR stock, in good condition. After servicing the tank, and in particular oiling up or greasing bare metal surfaces and so on, the tank was wrapped in a special fabric cladding which, once complete and sealed, was attached to a dehumidifier unit to remove unwanted moisture from the air in order to prevent rusting. Preparing a tank for storage, or indeed removing one from Dri-Clad, was a dull and time-consuming process, and was never popular with the crews.

Crazy Horse

In the 1980s, the British Army was operating a small number of up-armoured Centurions as target tanks on firing ranges. These were driven by volunteer drivers – a couple of the author's mates did this but he never felt the need – and engaged by inert warheads, typically 84mm Carl Gustav (and never by other tanks). In 1987 a project was initiated to replace these with a Chieftain, in order to have a more agile target tank which could be supported logistically. As it was intended to use it as a target for aerial as well as ground attack, the top as well as side armour was to be enhanced. Crucially, to remove any possibility of a crewman being injured, it was to be radio-controlled; this was named Project Crazy Horse.

One of the earliest tanks produced (00EB33) was used, and had its gun, radios, NBC pack and most of its ammunition and external stowage removed. Hydraulic rams were fitted into the driver's compartment to control steering, accelerator and brakes, and a colour video camera was installed in place of the driver's periscope. Trials were conducted at Larkhill, starting in April 1988, using 16-channel radio-control equipment supplied by Skyleader of Croydon. It was found that the tank could be controlled at ranges of up

to 10km, and in order to reduce the problem of a runaway tank if the control link was broken, the fuel capacity was limited to 35 litres, enough for only 3km of travel. Although it did not enter service, the tank provided useful data and now forms part of the reserve collection in the Tank Museum, Bovington.

Chieftain SID

In the mid-1980s two versions of a tank called SID – Signature Integration Demonstrator – were built around a Chieftain MBT. They were heralded as the world's first stealth tanks, rather than a mere concept demonstrator. They had to be able to perform in exactly the same manner as a service MBT, which made the designers work within sensible limits. The trials proved that it was able to reduce the radar, thermal imaging and acoustic signatures of the tank, the latter to such an extent that drivers who were used to changing gear by listening to the engine note found that they could not hear it well enough to do this.

Fire suppression system

Possibly the most interesting and esoteric

BELOW **The Crazy Horse Chieftain 00EB33.** *(TM 5023C2)*

proposal for the use of Chieftain was as a
fire suppression vehicle, to fight fires in high-
risk areas such as oilfields, well heads and
ammunition dumps. The proposal used two
Chieftains in tandem. One towed the other
using a rigid A-frame, the rearmost tank being
converted in order to carry a huge water
reservoir and pumping equipment. It appears
that the engine of the rear vehicle was to be
removed, and so the ensemble would be a
slow-moving beast, and would put even more
strain on the poor old L60. The lead vehicle
was manned by a driver plus one or two in the
turret, who operated the hose/water cannon
from under armour. Although there is no
evidence that the project was ever anything but
a 'paper panzer', and it is unknown who the
intended customer was, it remains probably
the most imaginative and outlandish use of
Chieftain ever.

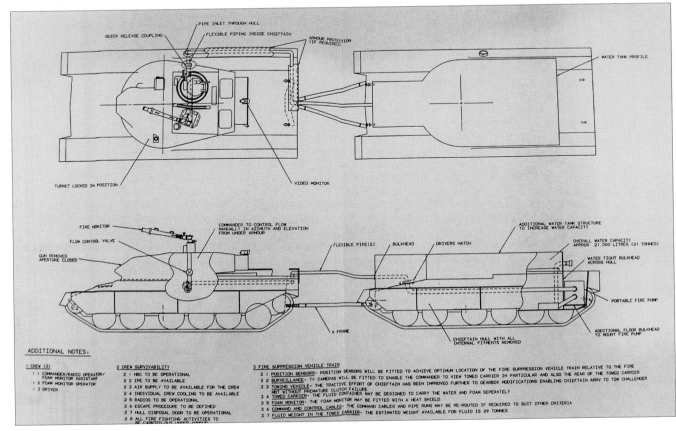

Appendix 1

Sources and bibliography

Primary

National Archives, Kew

Sources predominantly in the following document series: AVIA 37; BT11; CAB128, 148; DEFE13, 15, 24, 48, 70; FCO17, 39, 46; FO371; PREM13, 16; SUPP17; T225; WO32, 189, 194, 341, 404.

The Tank Museum, Bovington

The Archive and Library

Key documentation

Application of Fire from Chieftain Mk 1	AC 70407
Armoured Recovery Vehicle Chieftain FV4204	AC 61117
Chieftain AVRE Operating Information	2350-C-100-201
RAC Pamphlet 33 – Chieftain Armament	AC 71274
Servicing Schedule Chieftain (All Marks)	AC 61243
User Handbook for AVLB Chieftain	AC 60248
User Handbook for Tank Combat 120mm Gun Chieftain Mk 1	AC 14530
User Handbook for Tank Combat 120mm Gun Chieftain Mks 1, 2 and 3	AC 14908
User Handbook for Tank Combat 120mm Gun Chieftain Mk 5	AC 61034
User Handbook for Tank Combat 120mm gun Chieftain Mks 5–12	AC 62259

Secondary

Dunstan, Simon. *British Battle Tanks* (Arms & Armour, 1983).
—— *Centurion MBT* (Ian Allan, 1980).
—— *Chieftain MBT* (Osprey, 2003).
Forty, George. *Chieftain* (Ian Allan, 1979).
Foss, Christopher, and McKenzie, Peter. *The Vickers Tanks* (Keepdate, 1995).
Griffin, Rob. *Chieftain* (Crowood, 2001).
—— *Chieftain MBT* (Kagero, 2013).
Kneen, J.M. and Sutton, D.J. *The Craftsmen of the Army*, vol. 2 (Leo Cooper, 1996).
McKenzie, Peter. *The Barnbow Story* (Longhirst, 2000).
Macksey, Kenneth. *The Tanks 1945–1975* (Arms & Armour, 1979).
Mealor, R. and Axson, D.R. *REME Journal* (REME, 1974).
Ogorkiewicz, Richard. *Tanks: 100 Years of Evolution* (Osprey, 2015).
Suttie, William. *The Tank Factory* (History Press, 2015).
Taylor, Dick. *Challenger 1 Main Battle Tank* (Haynes, 2015).
Various. *International Defence Review*.
Various. *Jane's Armour & Artillery* (Jane's).
Various. *Jane's World Armies* (Jane's).
Various. *Royal Engineer Journal* 101 (1987).
Various. *The Tank Factory 1847–2014* (BAE Systems, 2013).
Various. *Tank Magazine* (RTR, 1962–96).

Appendix 2

Dimensions, capacities, details and data

Details refer to the original specification of the original Mk 2 tank: changes, modifications and upgrades are covered within the text.

Nomenclature

Designation:

Tank Combat 120mm Gun Chieftain

Dimensions

Length hull (front mudguard to gun crutch)	7.52m
Length gun front (muzzle to gun crutch)	10.8m
Length gun rear (front mudguard to gun muzzle in crutch)	9.75m
Height (to turret roof)	2.51m
Height (to top of commander's sight hood)	2.87m
Width (over tracks)	3.33m
Width (maximum)	3.66m
Ground clearance	0.51m
Mass (fully stowed but without crew)	52,435kg
Crew	4

Capacities

Fuel	1,772 litres
Coolant	132 litres
ME oil	114 litres
GUE oil	15.9 litres
Gearbox oil	43 litres
Final drive oil	45.7 litres (each)

Mobility

Maximum road speed	40.6km/h
Maximum reverse speed	9.8km/h
Vertical obstacle	0.9m
Maximum gradient	35°
Trench crossing	3.15m
Fording (unprepared)	1.07m
Bridge classification	56
Operating range	220km

Mobility

Powerpack	ME	Leyland L60 No 4 Mk 4A: 6-cylinder liquid-cooled 2-stroke CI multi-fuel.
	Bore	117.4mm
	Stroke	146.1mm
	Compression	16:1
	Power	650bhp (485kw) at 2,100rpm
	Transmission	David Brown Gear Industries TN12 Mk 3 gearbox, six forward and two reverse gears.
	Hydraulics	Gear changing (electro-hydraulic), steering, braking, lubrication.
	GUE	Coventry Climax H30 No 4 Mk 7A: 3-cylinder vertically opposed piston 2-stroke CI diesel.
Electrical system:		Four (two pairs) of 12v 100Ah lead acid hull batteries in series parallel giving 24v 200Ah. One pair of 12v 100Ah lead acid turret (radio) batteries in series giving 24v 100Ah.
		ME generator 150A.
		GUE generator 350A.
		Lights: head, side, tail, convoy, registration plate. Trailer socket on hull rear plate.
Fuel system		Four fuel tanks per side sponson, each containing a nylon-reinforced synthetic rubber fuel pannier; left side feeds GUE, right side ME, both via a gravity-fed base tank.
Wheels and suspension		Rear sprocket; six roadwheel pairs; front idler/track-adjuster wheel. Each roadwheel pair mounted on the stub axle of a Horstmann unit incorporating a top roller.
Tracks		610mm width, 159mm pitch-cast steel single dry pin. 96 links per side (new), 88 links per side (condemnation limit). Length on ground 4.78m.

Lethality and survivability

Armament	120mm L11A2 rifled gun, firing APDS, HESH and Smoke ammunition. 356mils (20°) elevation, –178mils (10°) depression. 53 projectiles.
	Browning .50in L21A1 RG, mounted coaxially with the MA. 600 rounds of flashing tip ammunition: L11A2 ammunition with four-dot sight, L13A1 with nine-dot sight.
	2 × 7.62mm GPMG, one mounted coaxially with the MA, one in the commander's cupola. 6,000 rounds of ammunition, loaded alternately ball and tracer.
Survivability	Cast turret and hull front; RHA welded plate elsewhere.
	36 charge container tubes in water jackets.
	2 × 66mm six-barrelled smoke grenade dischargers.
	No 2 NBC filtration and overpressure system.
	Powerpack fire warning alarm system; fixed and portable fire extinguishers.
	IR detection system.

Appendix 3

Abbreviations

ADS	Armour Delivery Squadron
AEV	Armoured Engineer Vehicle
AEV (G)	Armoured Engineer Vehicle (Gun)
AEV (W)	Armoured Engineer Vehicle (Winch)
AFV	Armoured Fighting Vehicle
APDS	Armour-Piercing Discarding Sabot
APFSDS	Armour-Piercing Fin-Stabilised Discarding-Sabot
APHE	Armour-Piercing High Explosive
ARRV	Armoured Repair and Recovery Vehicle
ARRV (P)	Armoured Repair and Recovery Vehicle (Persia)
ARV	Armoured Recovery Vehicle
ARV (J)	Armoured Recovery Vehicle (Jordan)
ATDU	Armour Trials and Development Unit (Bovington)
ATGW	Anti-Tank Guided Weapon
AV	Armoured Vehicle
AVLB	Armoured Vehicle Launched Bridge
AVRE	Armoured Vehicle Royal Engineers
BAEE	British Army Equipment Exhibition
BAOR	British Army of the Rhine
BATUS	British Army Training Unit Suffield
BL	Breech Loading
BML	Breech Mechanism Lever
BV	Boiling Vessel
CAA	Chieftain Additional Armour
CB	Circuit Breaker
CCMU	Commander's Control and Monitoring Unit (IFCS)
CE	Chemical Energy (ammunition)
CET	Combat Engineer Tractor
CFE	Conventional Forces Europe (Agreement)
CGC	Conspicuous Gallantry Cross
CHARRV	Chieftain Armoured Repair and Recovery Vehicle
CHAVRE	Chieftain Armoured Vehicle Royal Engineers
CI	Compression Ignition
CIM	Classroom Instructional Mounting
CIU	Computer & Interface Unit (IFSS)
CI-16	Cast Iron 16
CO	Commanding Officer
CoG	Centre of Gravity
CPU	Commander's Pressel Unit
CRARRV	Challenger Armoured Repair and Recovery Vehicle
CTR	Concept Test Rig
CV	Constant Velocity
D&M	Driving and Maintenance

DCGS	Deputy Chief of the General Staff
DFWES	Direct Fire Weapons Effects Simulator
DGFV	Director General Fighting Vehicles
DRAC	Director Royal Armoured Corps
DShK	Degtyaryov-Shpagin Large-Calibre (MG)
DS/T	Discarding Sabot Tracer
DTD	Department of Tank Design
ECE	Electrical Control Technicians
ERA	Explosive Reactive Armour
ESC	English Steel Castings
ESR	Electro-Slag Refined
ETW	Equipment Trials Wing
FHL	FH Lloyd
FIP	Fuel Injection Pump
FMR	Field Miniature Range
FMX	Fire and Manoeuvre Exercise
FNA	Firing Needle Assembly
FOO	Forward Operating Officer
FSAPDS	Fin-Stabilised Armour-Piercing Discarding Sabot
FTX	Field Training Exercise
FVRDE	Fighting Vehicle Research and Development Establishment (Chertsey) (to 1970)
GCE	Gun Control Equipment
GCP	Gear Controller Pedal
GE	General Electric
GEC	General Electric Company
GPMG	General-Purpose Machine Gun
GSR	General Staff Requirement
GTS	Gunnery Training Simulator
GUE	Generating Unit Engine
GV	Giant Viper
HE	High Explosive
HEAT	High Explosive Anti-Tank
HESH	High-Explosive Squash Head
HSS	Hydrostrut Suspension System
IC	Intercommunication
IDF	Israeli Defence Forces
IFCS	Improved Fire Control System
IGB	Inner German Border
II	Image Intensifier
IMS	International Military Services
IR	Infra-Red
ISD	In-Service Date

ITCH	Individual Tank Crewman's Heater		RHS	Right-Hand Side
KAPE	Keep the Army in the Public Eye		RMG	Ranging Machine Gun
KE	Kinetic Energy (ammunition)		RO	Royal Ordnance PLC
KL	K&L Steelfounders		ROFL	Royal Ordnance Factory Leeds
LAIC	Long Armour Infantry Course		RPG	Ruchnoy Protivotankovy Granatomyot, generally but inaccurately translated as Rocket-Propelled Grenade
LHS	Left-Hand Side			
LRF	Laser Rangefinder			
MA	Main Armament		RSM (I)	Regimental Sergeant Major (Instructor)
MBS	Muzzle Boresight		RTR	Royal Tank Regiment
MBSGD	Multi-Barrelled Smoke Grenade Discharger		SA cam	Semi-Automatic Cam
MBT	Main Battle Tank		Scots DG	Royal Scots Dragoon Guards
MC	Military Cross		SH/P	Squash Head Practice
MDBF	Mean Distance Between Failures		SHQ	Squadron Headquarters
ME	Main Engine		SID	Signature Integration Demonstrator
MG	Machine Gun		SIMFICS	Fire Simulator (IFCS)
MGO	Master-General of the Ordnance		SIMFIRE	Fire Simulator
MoD	Ministry of Defence		SLTA	Soltau-Lüneburg Training Area
MRS	Muzzle Reference System		SOS	Struck Off Strength
MV	Muzzle Velocity		SP	Special Projects
MVEE	Military Vehicles and Engineering Establishment (Chertsey) (from 1970)		Sqn	Squadron
			SSM	Squadron Sergeant Major
NAVAID	Navigation Set Land Vehicular		SU	Sight Unit
NBC	Nuclear, Biological and Chemical		TISH	Thermal Imager Sensor Head
NC/K	Nitro-Cellulose Kraft		TLS	Tank Laser Sight
OE	Operational Emergency		TOGS	Thermal Observation and Gunnery Sight
OP	Observation Post		Tp	Troop
OPFOR	Opposing Force		TVE	Tube Vent Electric
PM	Project Manager		UBRE	Unit Bulk Refuelling Equipment
PRI	Projector Reticule Image		VA	Vickers-Armstrong (Elswick)
PRV	Pressure Relief Valve		VDS	Vickers Defence Systems
PTO	Power Take-Off		VHF	Very High Frequency
QF	Quick Firing		VOR	Vehicle Off Road
QOH	Queen's Own Hussars		VRC	Vehicle Radio Communications
QRIH	Queen's Royal Irish Hussars		VT	Vent Tube
RA	Royal Artillery		VTL	Vent Tube Loader
RAC	Royal Armoured Corps		WMR	War Maintenance Reserve
RADIAC	Radiation detection		WO	War Office
RARDE	Royal Armament Research & Development Establishment (from 1984)		WOPS	War Office Policy Statement
			WP	White Phosphorous
RE	Royal Engineers		4/7DG	4th/7th Dragoon Guards
REME	Royal Electrical & Mechanical Engineers		13/18H	13th/18th King's Hussars
RG	Ranging Gun		14/20H	14th/20th King's Hussars
RH	Royal Hussars		15/19H	15th/19th King's Hussars
RHA	Rolled Homogenous Armour		16/5L	16th/5th Lancers
RHQ	Regimental Headquarters		17/21L	17th/21st Lancers

Index

firing circuits 66–8
firing handle 67
firing simulators 134–5
firing train 66
firing trials 57, 59–61
Fisher, Andy 50, 86–7, 100–1
FLEETFOOT programme 46
Flynn, Michael 132
fording 146
fuel gauge 49
fuel system 151
fuels 39–43
fume extractors 68–9
funnies 141–9

gear changing 38
gearbox 33, 38, 48–9
Germany, export sales 103
gun cradle 65–6
Gun Junction Box 67–8
gunner 33
    cleaning the MA 70
    firing of guns 67, 68
guns 10–15, 59–61, 151
    120mm 59–64
    fire control system
        improvements 74–6
    firing circuits 66–8

Hame, Lt Col Peter 89–90
Harrison, Capt Stephen 99
Hayden, Tpr Andy 50
heaters 138–9
HIGH NOON exercise 46
High-Explosive Squash Head 13
Hilton, Sgt Skip 100
Hockings, LCpl Bruce 98
Hopkinson, Maj Gen 16
Horstmann suspension 29, 41, 51
HOTSHOT exercises 105
Hutton, Maj Gen 103
hydraulic starting method 37
Hydrostrut suspension 141

Improved Fire Control System
    (IFCS) 76–7
Indian export sales 114
Individual Tank Crewman's Heater
    (ITCH) suits 139
infra-red (IR) equipment 80–3
IR (infra-red) equipment 80–3

Iran–Iraq War 109, 111
Iranian export sales 108–9, 115, 123–5
Iraqi export sales 113, 115, 125–6
Israel Defence Forces 7
Israeli export sales 105–7, 138
ITCH (Individual Tank Crewman's
    Heater) suits 139

Jacobs, Sgt Bob 31
Jordanian export sales 109–12, 115,
    125–6

K&L Steelfounders 50, 56
Korean War 11
Kuwaiti export sales 112–13, 115

L11 rifled gun 13
L60 engine 39–48
Larkspur radio system 84–5
laser rangefinders 73–4
Libyan export sales 107
Link-Miles driver trainer 134
liquid propellant guns 11–12
loader/radio operator 33
    cleaning the MA 70
loading guns 60–1
Lomax, Cpl 67
Longcross test track 20

McArthur, Major Iain 39
maintenance 90–2
Marksman 146
Mason, British Defence Minister
    Roy 114
May, Cpl Phil 85
MBSGD (Multi-Barrelled Smoke
    Grenade Dischargers) 77–8
MBT 80 programme 7
Mean Distance Between Failures
    (MDBF) 42, 46
MEDICINE MAN exercise 85
Merritt, Herbert 48
Meteor petrol engine 13
meteorological probes 77
Microflow Ltd 78
Middle East peace settlement 106–7
Military Vehicles and Engineering
    Establishment (MVEE) 39
mobility 28–30, 151
Moore, Cpl Alf 49
Muir, Maj John 98–9

Multi-Barrelled Smoke Grenade
    Dischargers (MBSGD) 77–8
Muzzle Boresight (MBS) 74
Muzzle Reference System (MRS) 74–6

Napper, Lt Col Mike 59
NATO 6–7
    multi-fuel engine policy 39–40
Navigation Set Land Vehicular system
    (NAVAID) 83, 85
NBC (nuclear, biological and chemical)
    protection 78–80
Neale, Tpr Smiler 100–1
Netherlands, export sales 103–4
New, Maj Gen Sir Laurence 6–7
night periscope 36
night-fighting equipment 80–3
No 11 vision cupola 70–1
No 15 Mk 1 cupola 70–1
No 36 periscope 33, 36
No 40 Mk 1 periscope 70, 72
normal firing circuit 66–7
nuclear, biological and chemical (NBC)
    protection 78–80

obdurators 65–6
    cleaning 70
obesity (of Chieftain tank) 30–3
O'Callaghan, Mr T. 39
Omani export sales 113–15
    120mm gun 59–61
    ammunition 61–64
Operation ABANET 97, 100
Operation DESERT SHIELD 130–1
operational mobility 28

Pakistani export sales 114
PALLOS exercise 20
Patterson, Maj Gen John 63
periscopes 33, 36, 70–2
Piper, Lt Col Warren 23
pistons 42–3
powerpacks 151
pre-production vehicle history 18–19
production 20–4
pusher bar 143

radiators 44
radio operator/loader 33
radio systems 84–5
radio-controlled tank 147–8